The **C**

Am

Portraiture

Today

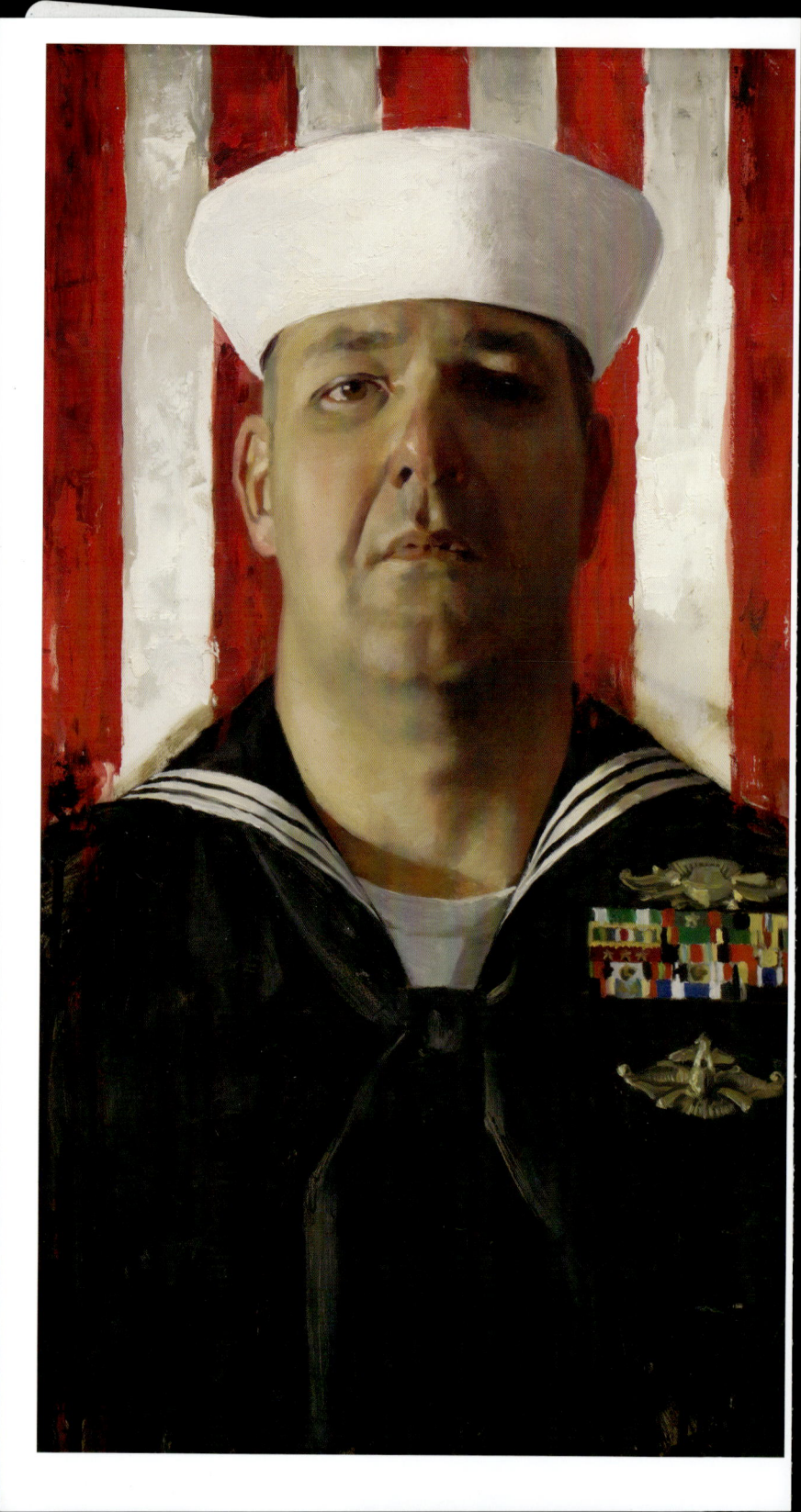

The Outwin 2019
American Portraiture Today

Outwin Boochever
Portrait Competition

National Portrait Gallery
Smithsonian Institution
Washington, D.C.

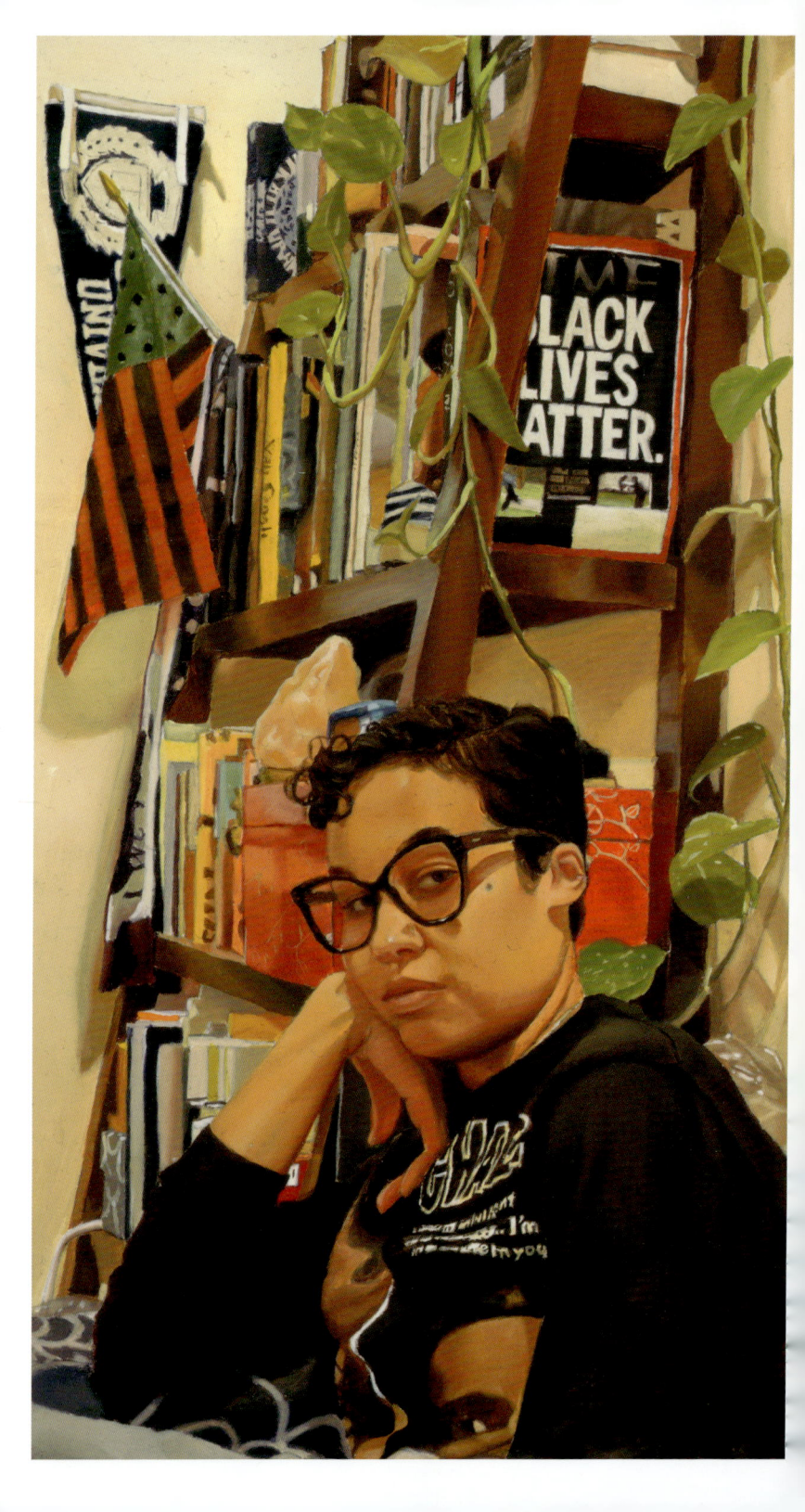

Contents

- 6   Foreword / *Kim Sajet*
- 9   An Appreciation: Virginia Outwin Boochever
- 11   Portraiture at an Intersection in History: The Fifth Triennial Outwin Boochever Portrait Competition / *Dorothy Moss*
- 23   Outwin Boochever Portrait Competition 2019
- 24   First Prize: HUGO CROSTHWAITE / *Taína Caragol*
- 26   Second Prize: SAM COMEN / *Taína Caragol*
- 28   Third Prize (tie): RICHARD GREENE and WAYDE McINTOSH / *Taína Caragol*
- 32   Commended Works
- 35   Competition Finalists
- 83   Jurors' Comments / *Taína Caragol, Brandon Brame Fortune, Harry Gamboa Jr., Lauren Haynes, Byron Kim, Dorothy Moss, Jefferson Pinder*
- 89   Acknowledgments
- 93   Previous Prize Winners
- 95   Index of Artists

Foreword

Kim Sajet, *Director, National Portrait Gallery*

Something fabulous happened in May 2018. For the first time since the Outwin Boochever Portrait Competition began, nearly fifteen years ago, the call for entries was reported by the Associated Press and made national news. Lauded as "highly prestigious" where the "stakes were high," the Outwin was credited with having "accelerated participants' careers." Suddenly, the National Portrait Gallery's triennial invitation to artists across the nation was gaining widespread recognition, and as a result, the museum received a record number of entries from artists working in every state of the U.S. and Puerto Rico. Suddenly, it seemed as if we had turned a corner, and our relatively young competition was earning a reputation for locating the best examples of American portraiture. Why?

      The explanation, I would like to suggest, is four-fold. First, since its inception in 2006, the Outwin has consistently chosen remarkable jurors from across the visual arts to select the most innovative portraitists from a blind selection. They ensure that it is not who the artists are but what they have created that counts. The competition has shown us that there are always new creatives to meet and surprising likenesses to admire.

      The second reason, I think, is the "legacy" of each exhibition. In addition to receiving a cash award, each first-prize winner of the Outwin Boochever Portrait Competition is granted the opportunity to take on a commission for the National Portrait Gallery. These artists create a portrait of a notable American, which not only enhances the collection but also strengthens the reputations of the artists, particularly with regard to acquisitions and exhibitions. After winning the first competition in 2006, artist David Lenz went on to paint a portrait of Eunice Kennedy Shriver for the museum's collection. That same year, Susanna Coffey was selected as a finalist, and her self-portrait was eventually acquired as well. Mequitta Ahuja, who was a finalist in 2009, was included in the National Portrait Gallery's exhibition *Portraiture Now: Drawing on the Edge* in 2012.

The third contribution to the Outwin Boochever Portrait Competition's growing appeal is the national tour that starting in 2016 introduced new communities to the best of contemporary portraiture. And, finally, as curator Dorothy Moss notes in her essay, Amy Sherald's portrait *Miss Everything (Unsuppressed Deliverance)* won first prize in 2016 and led to her having the opportunity to paint the official portrait of First Lady Michelle Obama. As the August 2019 issue of *Vogue* magazine notes: "Sherald's painting of the former First Lady is larger than life and gloriously untraditional," and it took the nation by storm after its unveiling in February 2018. The "Obama Effect" doubled the museum's attendance and cemented the competition's power to capture national attention.

At the end of the day, the secret ingredient is the powerful link between the art world and the real world, where contemporary issues around individuality and identity; creativity and community, come together to spark critical conversations. I have no doubt that the 2019 exhibition will push this even further, and this is a testament to the support of the Boochever family and the legacy of Virginia Outwin Boochever, who saw what we all now know: portraiture can change the world.

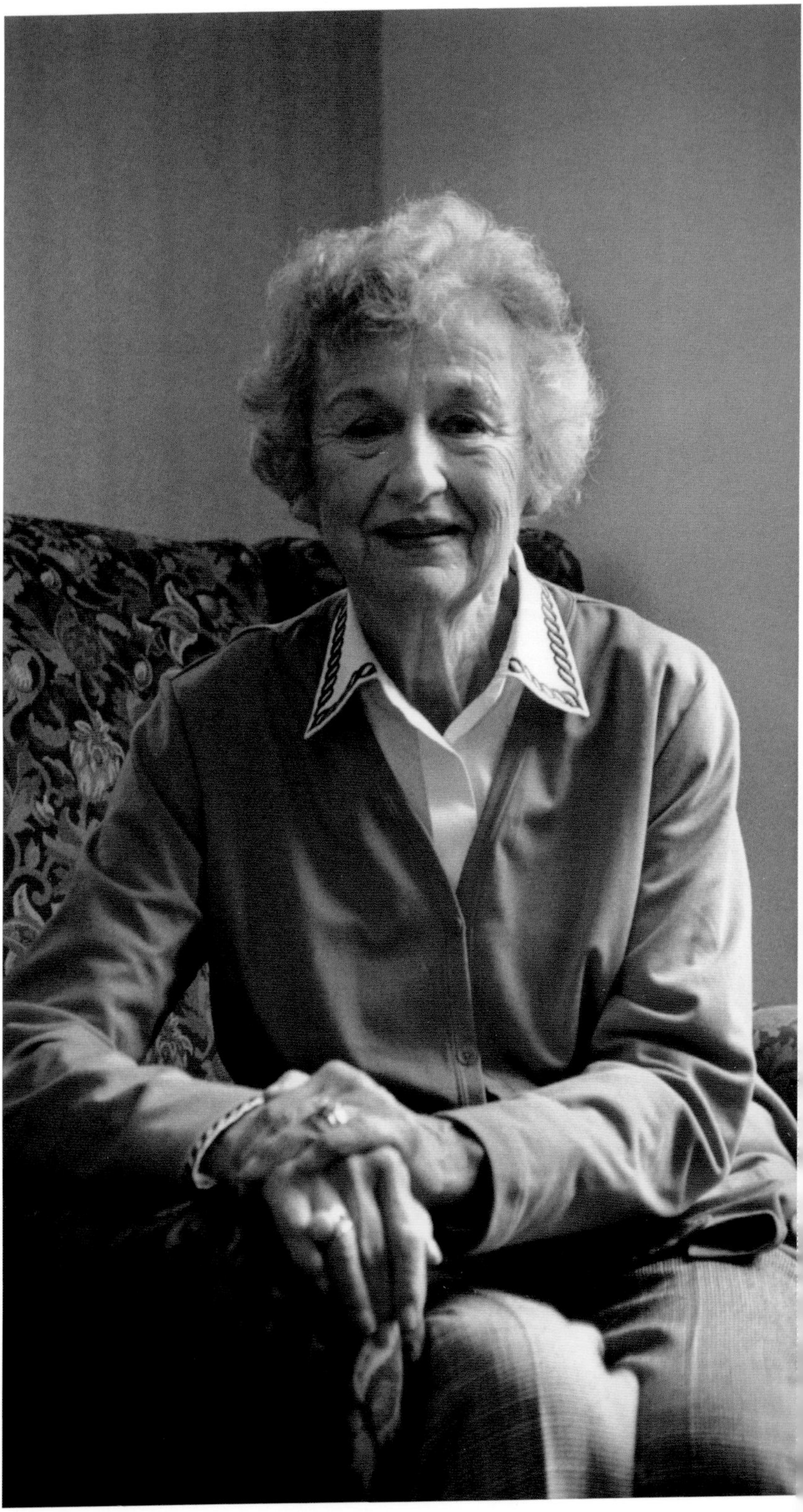

An Appreciation:

Virginia Outwin Boochever

Virginia Outwin Boochever (1920–2005) was born in Newark, New Jersey, and grew up in nearby Maplewood, where her father was the president of a medical supply company. After graduating from Smith College in 1941, she became one of the first female commissioned officers in the Navy WAVES. In 1945, she married Louis C. Boochever Jr., a U.S. Foreign Service officer, and for the next thirty years, she dedicated herself to raising four children and to the diplomatic life that took the family to Luxembourg, Paris, Belgrade, Rome, and Brussels. Gregarious and curious, she took pleasure in learning about the art and culture of the countries where she lived and engaging the myriad people she met.

In 1974, the Boochevers moved to Washington, D.C., where Mrs. Boochever took on a variety of volunteer activities. She was most passionate, however, about her work as a docent at the National Portrait Gallery. Appreciation of art was a lifelong interest: as a young woman she had studied art at the graduate level, and she and her husband were enthusiastic collectors. For nearly two decades, Mrs. Boochever delighted National Portrait Gallery visitors with her knowledge of the artworks, especially of the subjects' lives and times. She moved to Brunswick, Maine, in 2003.

Always interested in people, Mrs. Boochever saw the endowment of a portrait competition at the National Portrait Gallery as a way to benefit artists directly. Her knowledge of the portrait museums of England and Australia allowed her to understand the role that their competitions play in encouraging portraiture, and she saw the endowment as a unique opportunity to fill a void in the American art world.

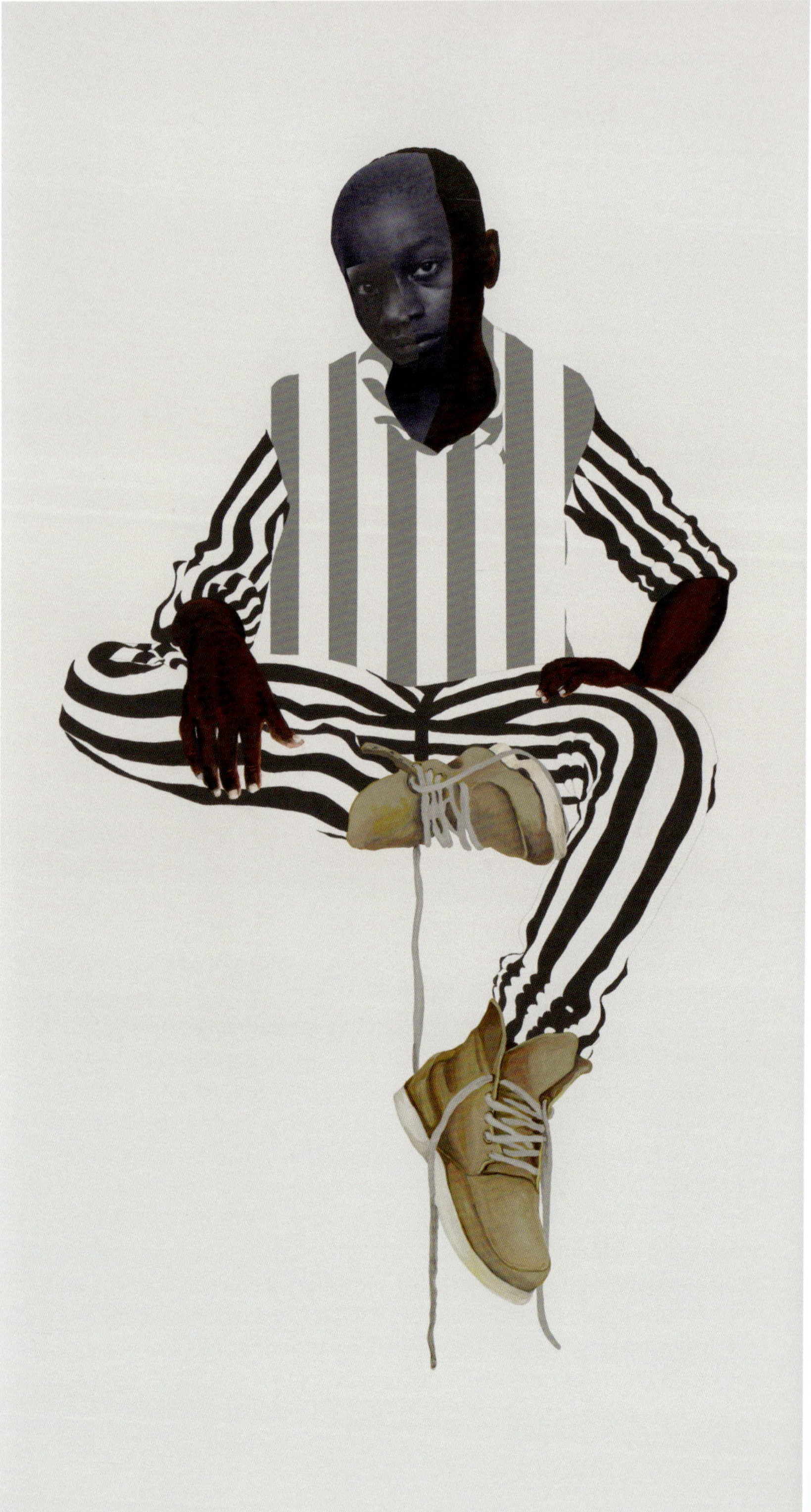

Portraiture at an Intersection in History:

The Fifth Triennial Outwin Boochever Portrait Competition

Dorothy Moss, *Curator of Painting and Sculpture, and Director, Outwin Boochever Portrait Competition, National Portrait Gallery*

The unveiling of the National Portrait Gallery's official portraits of President Barack Obama and First Lady Michelle Obama on February 12, 2018, marked a watershed moment in the history of art (fig. 1). The paintings reinvigorated critical discussions around portraiture on an international level and transformed the National Portrait Gallery as an institution. The museum's attendance doubled, and its profile, along with those of the commissioned artists, Kehinde Wiley and Amy Sherald, reached new heights.

     Sherald is now widely recognized for her work on the portrait of Michelle Obama, but she is also a part of the story of the National Portrait Gallery's remarkable triennial. As an emerging artist working in Baltimore, she entered her painting *Miss Everything (Unsuppressed Deliverance)* in the 2016 Outwin Boochever Portrait Competition, where it won first prize (fig. 2). In addition to a $25,000 cash award, the Outwin grants its winners a commission. After winning the competition, Sherald was placed on the list of artists for the Obamas to consider, and Mrs. Obama selected Sherald to paint her official portrait. The first lady then became the subject of Sherald's first-prize commission.

     Since its inception in 2006, the Outwin has contributed to the resurgence of portraiture as a vital contemporary art form, and it has earned a formidable reputation for recognizing artists who are working at the forefront of the genre. This year, following the Obama portrait unveiling and several critically acclaimed exhibitions devoted to portraiture, there was a high level of anticipation as the museum's curators looked forward to discovering what the entries would reveal.[1]

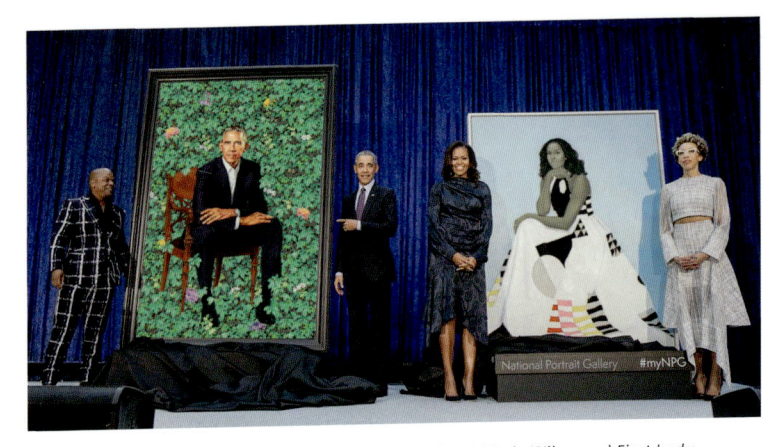

fig. 1. Unveiling of *President Barack Obama*, by Kehinde Wiley, and *First Lady Michelle Obama*, by Amy Sherald, on February 12, 2018

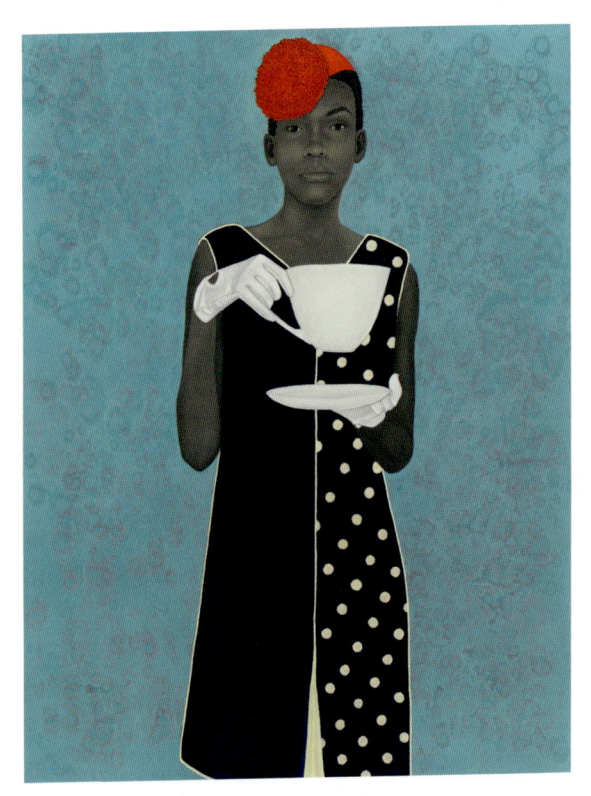

fig. 2. Amy Sherald (2016 first-prize winner), *Miss Everything (Unsuppressed Deliverance)*, 2013, Oil on canvas, 137.2 × 109.5 cm (54 × 43 ⅛ in.), Collection of Frances and Burton Reifler

In 2016, it was Sherald who stunned the jury with her fresh and energizing painting *Miss Everything*. The portrait reminded us of the work of Barkley Hendricks and Kerry James Marshall, but it was not derivative. We knew we had found an artist who was tapping into the future of portraiture because the subject was so unforgettable in its forward-facing, hopeful view of the African American experience. The day after the jury viewed the work, art historian Helen Molesworth commented on the effect of *Miss Everything*: "I can't stop thinking about that insouciant girl." None of us could.

Like Sherald, the artists who were selected for inclusion in the 2019 Outwin exhibition are thoughtful about the history of representation and insistent upon the presence of the subject in their work. Their portraits reflect the current moment, and many evoke a strong sense of activism rooted in empathy. Some approach the genre through conceptual means, while others adhere to a more traditional framework, but all forty-six of these portraits touch on topics that were frequently referenced in the more-than 2,600 entries that we received. And, for the first time in the competition's history, the call for entries specifically asked artists to respond "to the current political and social context." The sitters' stories relate to issues that are regularly covered on the news today, such as the status of American workers, the nation's housing crisis, LGBTQ+ rights, Black Lives Matter, the youth movement against gun violence, and immigration.

Furthermore, because the guidelines no longer require portraits to be made from a direct encounter between the artist and the sitter, this exhibition includes portraits of historical figures. An exquisite drawing by Lava Thomas portrays Lottie Green Varner, one of over eighty African American civil rights workers who was arrested during the Montgomery Bus Boycott in February 1956 (see p. 80). Deborah Roberts's portrait responds to the life of George Stinney Jr. (1929–1944), who was executed at age fourteen for a crime he did not commit (see p. 10, p. 71). These artists engage the past to restage history, visualizing a narrative that is brave and inclusive, as well as messy and troubling.

This year's first-prize winner, Hugo Crosthwaite, who works in San Diego and Tijuana, is amplifying the role of portraiture at a critical time in the history of border politics. In his work *A Portrait of Berenice Sarmiento Chávez*, he honors the experiences of a woman who has crossed the border to look for a better life in the United States (see p. 25). His sensitive portrayal of her struggles is a profound tribute to those like her who have risked everything for their own safety and that of their families. It seems clear that the future of portraiture is with artists who, in the face of suffering, demonstrate resilience and strength through creativity and hope.

By encouraging artists to submit works that responded to current issues, and by accepting portraits made in a variety of media, this year's Outwin aimed to expand the scope of portraiture and highlight the genre's relevance in the contemporary art world. Paintings, drawings, photographs, and sculptures are displayed alongside time-based media and installation art. And, for the first time, the jurors selected a performance piece: *Portrait: No. 1 Man* by Sheldon Scott, which comments on the grueling forced labor of the enslaved people in coastal regions of the pre-Civil War South (see pp. 74–75).

It is important to consider the evolution of the Outwin and the modifications to the competition in light of institutional goals and shifts in contemporary art. Yet even with the changes that have been necessary over time to ensure the relevance of the program, the Outwin has not diverged from the spirit in which it was founded. The common thread through the years is the vision of its remarkable benefactor, Virginia Outwin Boochever (1920–2005).

Mrs. Boochever was one of the first women commissioned officers in the Navy WAVES who lived a life of service with her husband Louis C. Boochever, a U.S. Foreign Service officer. The couple's diplomatic work took them, along with their four children, to Luxembourg, Paris, Belgrade, Rome, and Brussels. With a global perspective on history, portraiture, and identity, Mrs. Boochever later brought her experiences to bear on her work as a National Portrait Gallery docent, a role she fulfilled for nearly two decades. She understood and believed in the transformative power of portraiture. Her deep passion for the way history and biography converge in portraiture and the genre's continued relevance in the contemporary world made her the perfect partner in realizing a strategic goal for the museum.

The Outwin Boochever Portrait Competition and exhibition commenced in 2006, with a sole focus on painting and sculpture and with a mandate for work that was the result of a direct encounter between artist and subject. With each subsequent iteration of the Outwin, the Portrait Gallery has taken stock of how portraiture has shifted within the previous three years. The triennial provides an opportunity for us to pause, look back, and envision where portraiture is headed. While our evolving institutional interests and priorities compel us to revise elements of the process, there are two questions that consistently drive our work: How does the National Portrait Gallery make this particular art competition and its resulting exhibition, which travels across the country, relevant and compelling? And, how does this exhibition contribute to the current production of portraiture as a guidepost for the future of the genre? These questions, along with what drives artists to enter the Outwin, are on the minds of the curators and invited jurors as they also consider the broader developments in contemporary art, today's scholarship on portraiture, and the interests of the general public. As a consequence, each exhibition forms its own distinct identity.

In the catalogue for the inaugural Outwin Boochever Portrait Competition, Marc Pachter, who was then the National Portrait Gallery's director, discusses the origins of the competition as having been rooted in his strategic plan for the museum. He describes having wanted to develop a competition similar to the BP Award hosted by the National Portrait Gallery in London:

When I was asked to serve as director of the National Portrait Gallery, more than six years ago, the very first thing that came to mind as a goal was to create a national portrait competition. That hope had its origin in my enjoyment of the competition organized by our sister museum in London, which had managed to make the idea of portraiture exciting again after years of languishing in the shadow of other art forms.[2]

Pachter appointed Brandon Brame Fortune, who was then associate curator of painting and sculpture, to lead the charge in developing this exciting new initiative. Through her deep knowledge of the history of portraiture, her careful research of existing art competitions, and her conversations with museum professionals and with Virginia Outwin Boochever, Fortune created a dynamic program that has grown into a significant art world event. She now serves as the museum's chief curator and articulates that she has always kept the artists' needs at the forefront of the competition and exhibition, never wanting to burden those who entered with financial obligations. It was a daunting but rewarding task. "One of the biggest challenges for a national competition in the U.S. was the potential for shipping expenses for some works of art to be overwhelming for the artists we wanted to attract. Mrs. Boochever's generous gift has allowed those costs to be completely covered for all of the semi-finalists."[3]

Over the years, Fortune has been a guiding force of the Outwin. She has served on every jury, witnessing and influencing the shift in the landscape of American portraiture. In her comments for the 2006 catalogue, she hints at where she envisions the competition will take the Portrait Gallery over time. Describing how she imagines artists will counter the increasingly homogenous culture in advertising and mass media, she writes:

Contemporary artists have responded by creating subtle, careful portraits of individuals and by using depictions of the human body to explore complex issues of identity. The mark of their success is that we, as viewers, are curious about their subjects. We look long and hard, intrigued and hoping to discover more.[4]

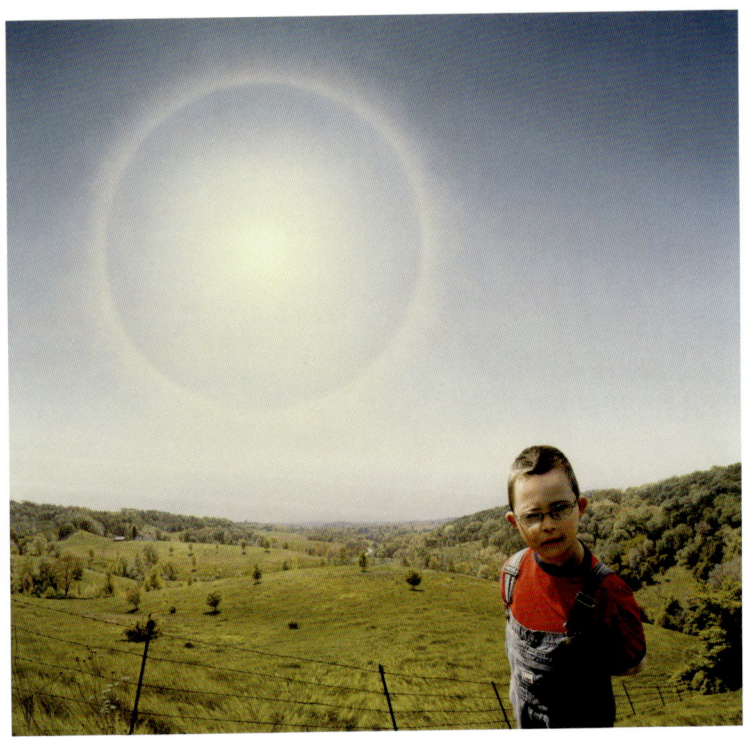

fig. 3. David Lenz (2006 first-prize winner), *Sam and the Perfect World*, 2005, Oil on linen, 44 × 46 in. (111.8 × 116.8 cm), Milwaukee Art Museum; purchase, with funds from the Linda and Daniel Bader Foundation, Suzanne and Richard Pieper, and Barbara Stein

That year, David Lenz won for *Sam and the Perfect World*, a portrait of his son that speaks to the challenges of having Down syndrome (fig. 3). "Sam is the opposite of the idealized 'perfect' countryside," Lenz observes. "Nevertheless, I think he has something very important to say."[5]

In reviewing the 2006 remarks, there is a shared feeling of surprise among the jurors (art historians Trevor Fairbrother, Thelma Golden, and Katy Siegel, and artist Sidney Goodman). The palpable sense of a new direction for the National Portrait Gallery as an institution and, more generally, for contemporary portraiture, is also evident in the jurors' reflections. Siegel summed up the jury's response:

Now that the painted portrait of prominent individuals has been replaced by photography and TV, museums like the National Portrait Gallery are reassessing not only their institutional mission but the meaning of portraiture itself. In the field of contemporary art, what was once an official genre of academic painting has lost its distinct character. What remains is a desire for direct contact between artist, subject, and viewer. Without institutional support or constraints, it is an open question how artists will choose to define and express this content.[6]

This theme of witnessing an institutional and art world shift continued into the subsequent competitions through the comments of the invited jurors — always an impressive cohort of critics, curators, and artists. While the names of the jurors may reveal a virtual "who's who" of the contemporary art world, many of them comment on what makes this competition stand apart from and push against what has been described as the "clubbiness" of some of the most visible contemporary art shows, such as the Whitney Biennial.[7] Jerry Saltz addressed this in his remarks after participating in the 2016 competition:

I love the Outwin Boochever Portrait Competition because it's open to anyone. This is like a social network. We are seeing anyone who self-identifies as a portrait artist entering the competition, not just the top one or two artists in the art world or just amateurs . . . This is everyone. This is a real competition, which makes it a real show.[8]

As Saltz notes, the openness of the competition buoys its authenticity, and in addition to welcoming new artists with each open call, the museum invites a new set of guest jurors for each iteration. The nature of the program thus allows for varied concepts of portraiture to form and new interpretations of the genre to emerge. The jurors' own work and their engagement with one another during the selection process shape the resulting exhibitions, while the vision of the National Portrait Gallery's current director, Kim Sajet, sets the tone. Sajet's championing of new approaches to portraiture, her support of the IDENTIFY performance art series, and her openness to experimentation have largely influenced the current installation.

In 2009, the competition began accepting entries beyond painting and sculpture. By opening itself up to photographs, drawings, prints, mixed media works, and time-based art, the Outwin presented a new view of how the genre was developing. That year, the top prize went to Dave Woody for a photograph of one of his graduate school friends (fig. 4). Entitled *Laura*, Woody's inkjet print has the look and feel of a painting by a Netherlandish Old Master. His was not the only portrait to engage with art history, and juror Wanda Corn observed:

As an art historian, I was pleased to see how many works self-consciously referenced portraiture of the past. Today's artists clearly know their art history, be it portraits by van Eyck, van der Weyden, Rembrandt, Rubens, or Ingres. It is nice to think that the teaching of art history may play a hand in educating today's figure painters.[9]

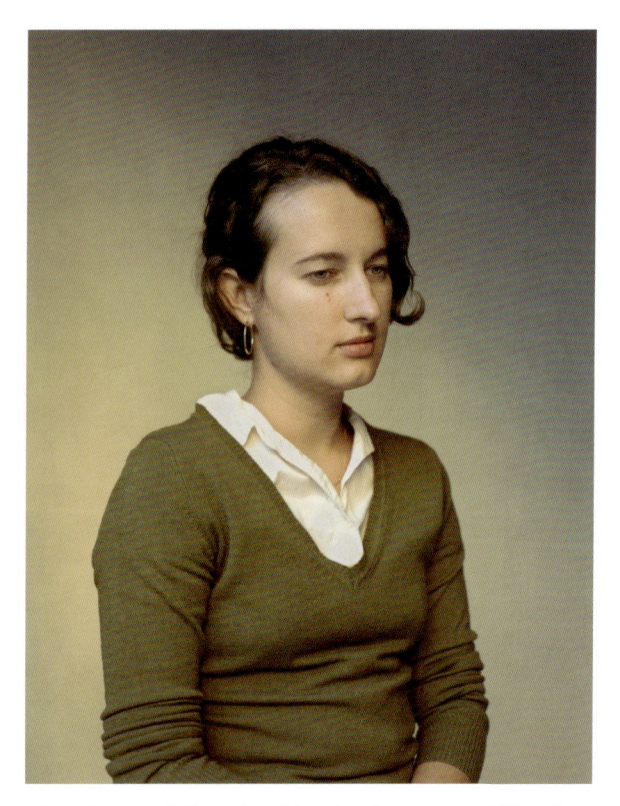

fig. 4. Dave Woody (2009 first-prize winner), *Laura*, 2007, Inkjet print, 81.3 × 63.5 cm (32 × 25 in.), Collection of the artist

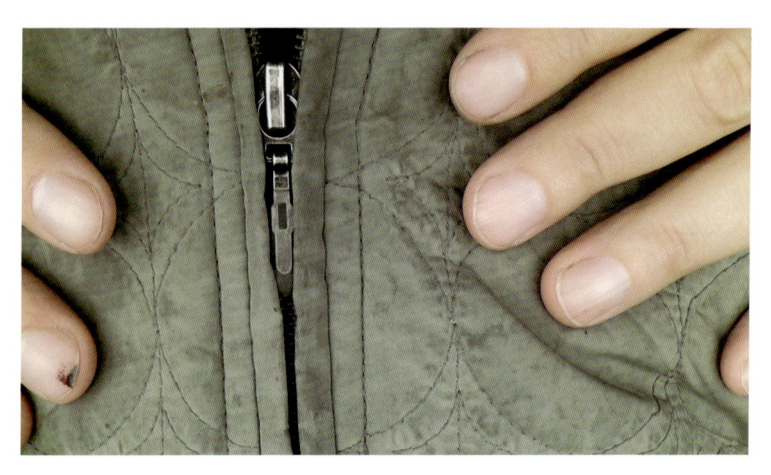

fig. 5. Bo Gehring (2013 first-prize winner), *Jessica Wickham*, 2010, HD video, 5:05 min., Collection of the artist

The 2013 Outwin, by contrast, was less about looking back and more about testing boundaries. Artists that year tended to expand upon the very concept of portraiture by employing new materials and embracing innovation. The jury was impressed by the levels of experimentation among the entries, particularly in the time-based media works. As one juror, the photographer Alec Soth, commented, "One thing that was really notable about this whole process was how strong the video was, and that was unexpected. It was so fresh and so alive."[10] In fact, both the first prize and the second prize that year went to time-based media artists, with Bo Gehring winning for his haunting portrait of precision woodworker Jessica Wickham (fig. 5). The subject's emotional response to her favorite piece of music, Arvo Pärt's "Cantus in Memoriam Benjamin Britten," is captured in a five-minute video. The camera moves in time with the music, and the imagery shifts from the area below the subject's feet to her body and, eventually to the space above her head. The result is a mesmerizing portrait that the *Washington Post* critic Philip Kennicott elaborates on in his discussion of portraiture's limitations:

Here it is, the body, the subject, in all its detail. Is there anything else? Nothing more? Accepting the limits of our knowledge is one of the essential humilities of being human, and Gehring's work dramatizes those limits. There is also a happy accident in the choice of music: Pärt's composition consists of slowly repeated descending scales, while Gehring's camera works up from the toes to the head. Taken together, these two metaphors of up and down, applied in different media, demonstrate how arbitrary most of our metaphors for measuring and defining human existence are, including the conceit that humans have both surface and depth.[11]

Rather than continuing this focus on experimentation, the 2016 jurors chose to concentrate on the dynamic between the artist and the subject. The resulting exhibition presented an intimate view of portraiture, which Dawoud Bey beautifully summarizes in his juror comments:

For me, the portrait works most effectively when it ceases to be merely an object or representation and becomes an actual experience of the individual described in the portrait. It is and remains a painting. It is and remains a photograph, but at some point if the portrait is doing what I hope it would do, one goes beyond the object to the experience of the individual and begins to have an emotional and psychological experience that's driven by the object.[12]

It was this definition that led us to select Amy Sherald's *Miss Everything (Unsuppressed Deliverance)*. Not only was Sherald's use of color and composition compelling, but the way the young subject engages directly with the viewer, with her hopeful expression and self-assuredness, stopped us in our tracks.

Remarkably, the portraits that stood out to the jury in 2019 were those that not only answered the call to address our current moment but those that also went a step further to serve as a kind of wake-up call, a call to action for all of us to take stock of our responsibilities to each other as human beings. This responsibility is captured on an individual level in every one of the forty-six selected works.

The majority of the portraits in *The Outwin 2019* represent people who are vulnerable. We meet immigrants who have crossed the border between the United States and Mexico looking for a better and safer life (see Hugo Crosthwaite, p. 25; Ruth Leonela Buentello, p. 43, and Patrick Martinez, p. 68). We come across unaccompanied minors whose portraits were painted when they were seeking shelter in and around Los Angeles, (see Kate Capshaw, pp. 46–47). And LGBTQ+ refugees are portrayed in a video by Shimon Attie and in a painting by Carla Crawford. Also included among the finalists are portraits of figures who are known for promoting social justice, such as DeRay Mckesson, a prominent activist for Black Lives Matter (see Quinn Russell Brown, p. 42); Bryan Stevenson, the founder and executive director of the Equal Justice Initiative (see Joshua Cogan, p. 49); and John Ahearn, an artist who demonstrates the power of portraiture through his community work (see Devon Rodriguez, p. 73). The exhibition also represents some of the young activists who, in the wake of the horrific school shootings in the United States, are leading the movement against gun violence (see Sandra Steinbrecher, p. 77).

I have had the privilege of co-curating *The Outwin 2019: American Portraiture Today* with my colleague Taína Caragol. We are proud that this exhibition is not about reaffirming the status and power of those who already are in positions of influence and control. Instead, it is about recognizing those who seek the simple and basic rights of safety, visibility, and respect as individuals, and those who enable those human rights through activism. *The Outwin 2019* is, therefore, about all of us. It is a reminder that in a time of division, the most powerful — even resilient — act is to see each other and to be seen.

Notes

1. In the past three years alone, a large number of solo exhibitions have featured pioneers in the art of portraiture, such as Kerry James Marshall (2009 Outwin Boochever Portrait Competition juror), whose 2016 multicity retrospective, organized by Helen Molesworth (2016 Outwin Boochever Portrait Competition juror), was a seminal exhibition of the decade in terms of its insistence on what Marshall has described as "putting blackness in art history." Dushko Petrovich, "The New Face of Portrait Painting," *T (The New York Times Style Magazine)*, February 12, 2018. Other pivotal and critically acclaimed exhibitions include *Martin Wong: Human Instamatic* at the Bronx Museum (2015), *Jordan Casteel: Nights in Harlem* at Casey Kaplan (2017), *Alice Neel, Uptown*, organized and curated by critic Hilton Als at David Zwirner (2017), *Front Room: Njideka Akunyili Crosby | Counterparts* at the Baltimore Museum of Art (2018), and the presentation of *The Birmingham Project* by Dawoud Bey (2016 Outwin Boochever Portrait Competition juror) at the National Gallery of Art, Washington, D.C. (2018). Group exhibitions have also focused on conceptual portraiture, including the National Portrait Gallery's *UnSeen: Our Past in a New Light, Ken Gonzales-Day and Titus Kaphar* (2018) and the Contemporary Jewish Museum's *Show Me as I Want to Be Seen* (2019). And, there is no shortage of significant recent critical writing on contemporary portraiture by artists and critics; see for example, the writings of Teju Cole, Dawoud Bey, Hilton Als, Darby English, and Jerry Saltz (2016 Outwin Boochever Portrait Competition juror).

2. Marc Pachter, Foreword in *The Outwin Boochever Portrait Competition 2006*, exhibition catalogue (Washington, D.C.: National Portrait Gallery, 2006), 6.

3. Brandon Brame Fortune, discussion with Dorothy Moss, June 17, 2019.

4. Brandon Brame Fortune, "Jurors' Comments" in *The Outwin Boochever Portrait Competition 2006*, exhibition catalogue (Washington, D.C.: National Portrait Gallery, 2006), 18.

5. "First Prize Winner: Sam and the Perfect World by David Lenz," in *The Outwin Boochever Portrait Competition 2006*, exhibition catalogue (Washington, D.C.: National Portrait Gallery, 2006), 20.

6. Katy Siegel, "Jurors' Comments" in *The Outwin Boochever Portrait Competition 2006*, exhibition catalogue (Washington, D.C.: National Portrait Gallery, 2006), 19.

7. For example, in Jonathan Yau's review of the 2019 Whitney Biennial, he concludes, "Despite the inclusiveness represented by these numbers, there is a clubbiness emanating from the 2019 Biennial that seems to hold true for every Biennial, with its coastal bias and disinclination to look beyond familiar schools, galleries, and institutional affiliations. As with earlier Biennials, various 'Exclusion Acts' are still in place." Jonathan Yau, "How Do Artists Get into the Whitney Biennial?" June 9, 2019, *Hyperallergic*. hyperallergic.com.

8. Jerry Saltz, "Jurors' Comments" in *The Outwin 2016: American Portraiture Today*, exhibition catalogue (Washington, D.C.: National Portrait Gallery, 2016), 20–21.

9. Wanda M. Corn, "Jurors' Comments" in *The Outwin Boochever Portrait Competition 2009*, exhibition catalogue (Washington, D.C.: National Portrait Gallery, 2009), 19.

10. Alec Soth, "Jurors' Comments" in *The Outwin Boochever Portrait Competition 2013*, exhibition catalogue (Washington, D.C.: National Portrait Gallery, 2013), 23.

11. Philip Kennicott, "Boochever Portrait Competition Winners," *Washington Post*, March 22, 2013.

12. Dawoud Bey, "Jurors' Comments" in *The Outwin 2016: American Portraiture Today*, exhibition catalogue (Washington, D.C.: National Portrait Gallery, 2016), 19.

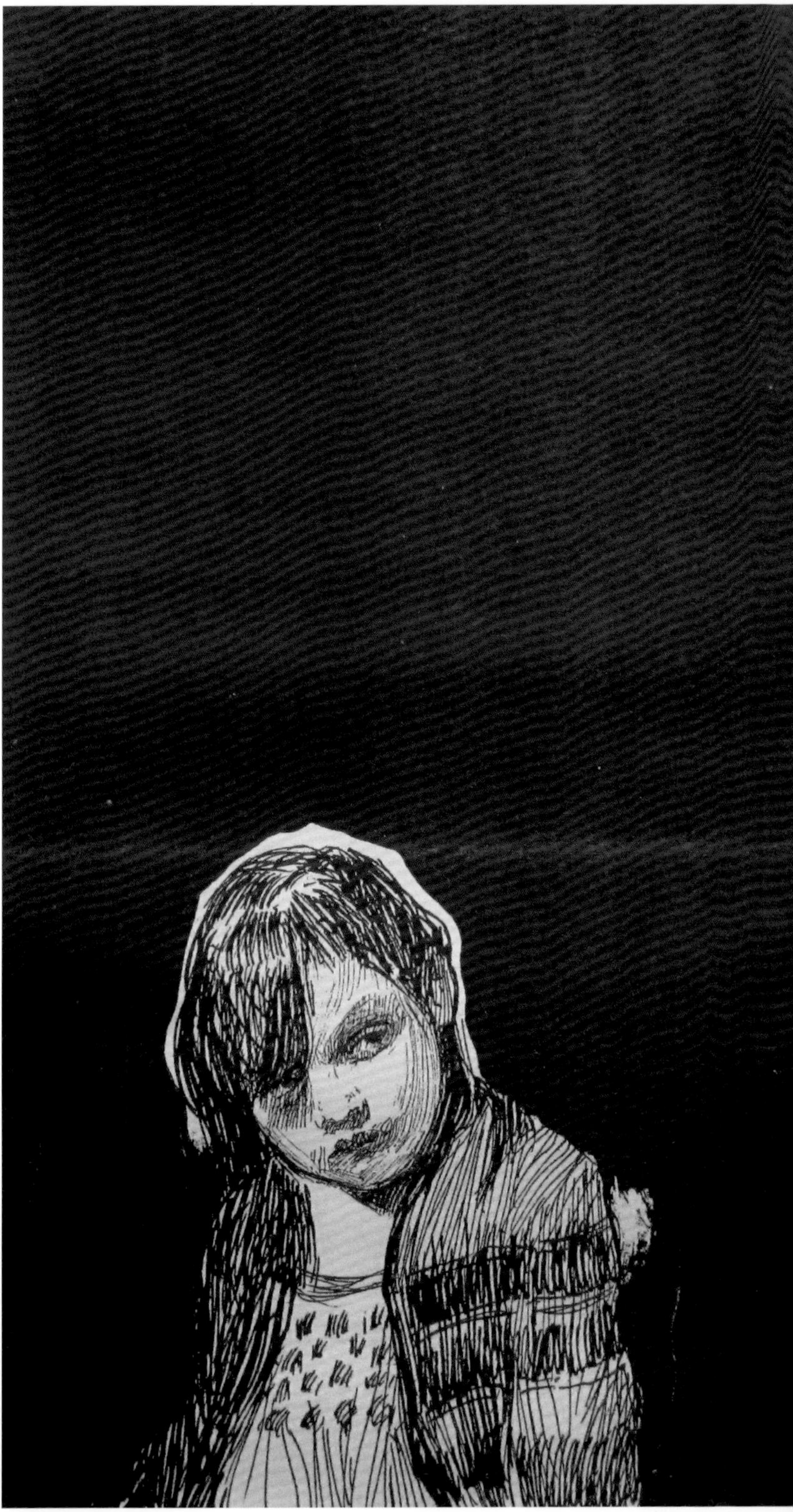

Outwin Boochever Portrait Competition 2019

Prize Winners

First Prize: HUGO CROSTHWAITE ($25,000)
plus a commission to create a portrait of a well-known living American for the National Portrait Gallery's collection

Second Prize: SAM COMEN ($7,500)

Third Prize (tie): RICHARD GREENE / WAYDE McINTOSH ($5,000)

Commended Artists:
NATALIA GARCÍA CLARK ($1,000)
LAUREN HARE ($1,000)
ADRIAN OCTAVIUS WALKER ($1,000)

Jurors

TAÍNA CARAGOL, curator of painting and sculpture and Latino art and history, National Portrait Gallery, Washington, D.C.

BRANDON BRAME FORTUNE, chief curator, National Portrait Gallery, Washington, D.C.

HARRY GAMBOA JR., artist, writer, and co-director of the program in photography and media, California Institute of the Arts, Valencia, CA

LAUREN HAYNES, curator of contemporary art, Crystal Bridges Museum of American Art, Bentonville, AR

BYRON KIM, artist and senior critic, Yale School of Art, New Haven, CT

DOROTHY MOSS, curator of painting and sculpture, National Portrait Gallery, Washington, D.C., and director, Outwin Boochever Portrait Competition

JEFFERSON PINDER, artist and professor of sculpture and contemporary practices, School of the Art Institute of Chicago

The National Portrait Gallery's fifth triennial Outwin Boochever Portrait Competition and its resulting exhibition highlight the excellence and innovation of today's most influential portraits. Artists over the age of eighteen who were living and working within the United States were eligible to enter between May 28 and September 7, 2018.

First Prize

Portraits have traditionally sought to capture the essence of a person by presenting the subject at a specific moment. Hugo Crosthwaite's animated short *A Portrait of Berenice Sarmiento Chávez* stands in sharp contrast to that precedent as it interweaves various memories, experiences, and aspirations of a young woman from Tijuana who decides to pursue the American Dream.

Set to the soundtrack of a dissonant guitar and a raspy voice singing in Spanish, the narrative begins with the formation of a black rectangular border, which serves to outline the hand-drawn vignettes that follow. A pair of eyes becomes the pensive gaze of a hopeful, idealistic Berenice Sarmiento Chávez. Ink and wash continue to fill the space, visually describing the subject's humble home while death lurks behind the door. Then, strokes of white paint transform her figure into a grotesque Mickey Mouse before she is completely obscured.

Applied by the invisible hand of the artist, black ink, gray wash, and white paint wipe out one scene to construct another that is then eradicated by blackness, as if by divine action or fate itself. The nervous lines and jumpy imagery work together to tell the story of a woman who travels north, narrowly escaping the lethal dangers of the immigration journey. Once in the land of Stars and Stripes, Berenice serves wealthy leering men, who hover dangerously close to her. Later, abundant white paint shoots from a gun, completely erasing her face. The blank page returns, and the figure of a small, innocent girl emerges. She appears both dreamy and weary until a tunnel of dark engulfs her and the music ends.

This video is part of a series based on Crosthwaite's interviews with people who are living in or are passing through his native Tijuana. The resultant improvised drawings represent the collective memories and oral histories from that part of the Mexico-United States border. The artist often addresses the chasm between everyday life in Tijuana and the city's international reputation as a place of lawlessness.

— Taína Caragol, *Curator of painting and sculpture and Latino art and history, National Portrait Gallery*

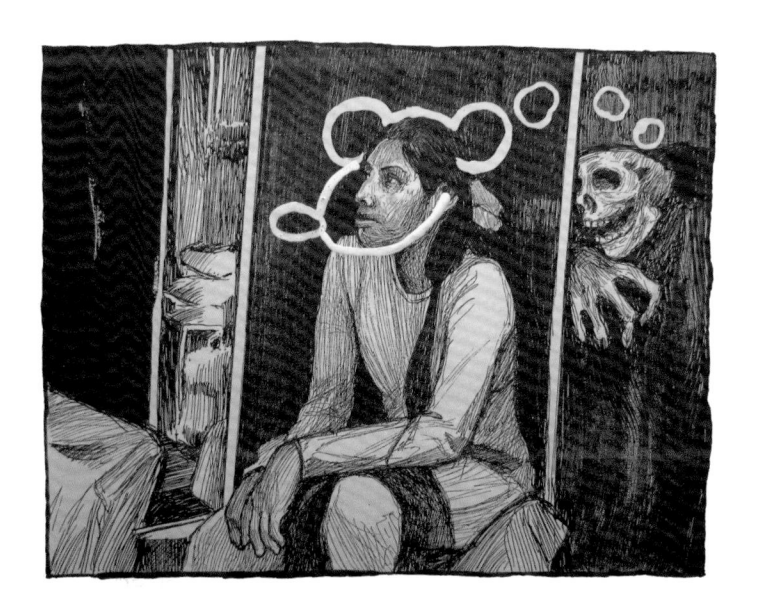

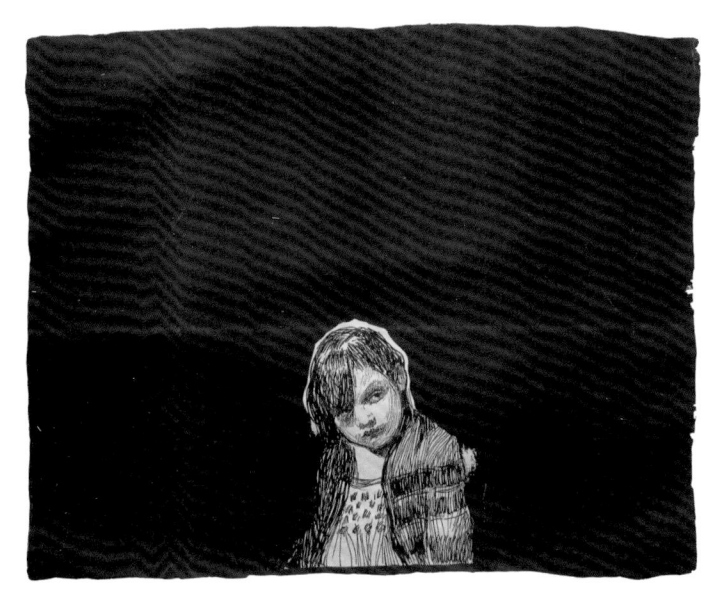

First Prize

A Portrait of Berenice Sarmiento Chávez

Hugo Crosthwaite (San Diego, California)
Stop-motion drawing animation (3:12 min.), 2018
Collection of the artist, courtesy of Luis De Jesus Los Angeles

Second Prize

Amidst a forest of stainless steel kitchen utensils and implements, a man poses for the camera in a clean white apron and a backwards baseball cap. He gazes slightly upwards and rests his right hand on the sink while projecting an air of dignity from the center of his professional domain.

This photograph is part of Sam Comen's series *Working America*, in which he documents and pays homage to the multicultural immigrant American workforce of his native Los Angeles. Comen follows in the tradition of August Sander, Irving Penn, and other twentieth-century photographers as he strives to make workers visible. His photographs of behind-the-scenes laborers, such as dishwashers, shoemakers, and tailors, acknowledge his sitters' contributions to society. The artist notes, "Through diligence, creativity, and entrepreneurial spirit, these new Americans seek a chance to better their lives and the lives of their children through the universally acknowledged mandate of rolling up their sleeves and going to work. None are asking for a free ride."

Comen is best known for his environmental portrait essays that feature evocative California locales. As a documentary photographer, he has long focused on themes of American identity, community-building, immigration, democracy, and social justice. In 2017, the National Portrait Gallery featured his photography in the exhibition *The Sweat of Their Face: Portraying American Workers*.

— Taína Caragol

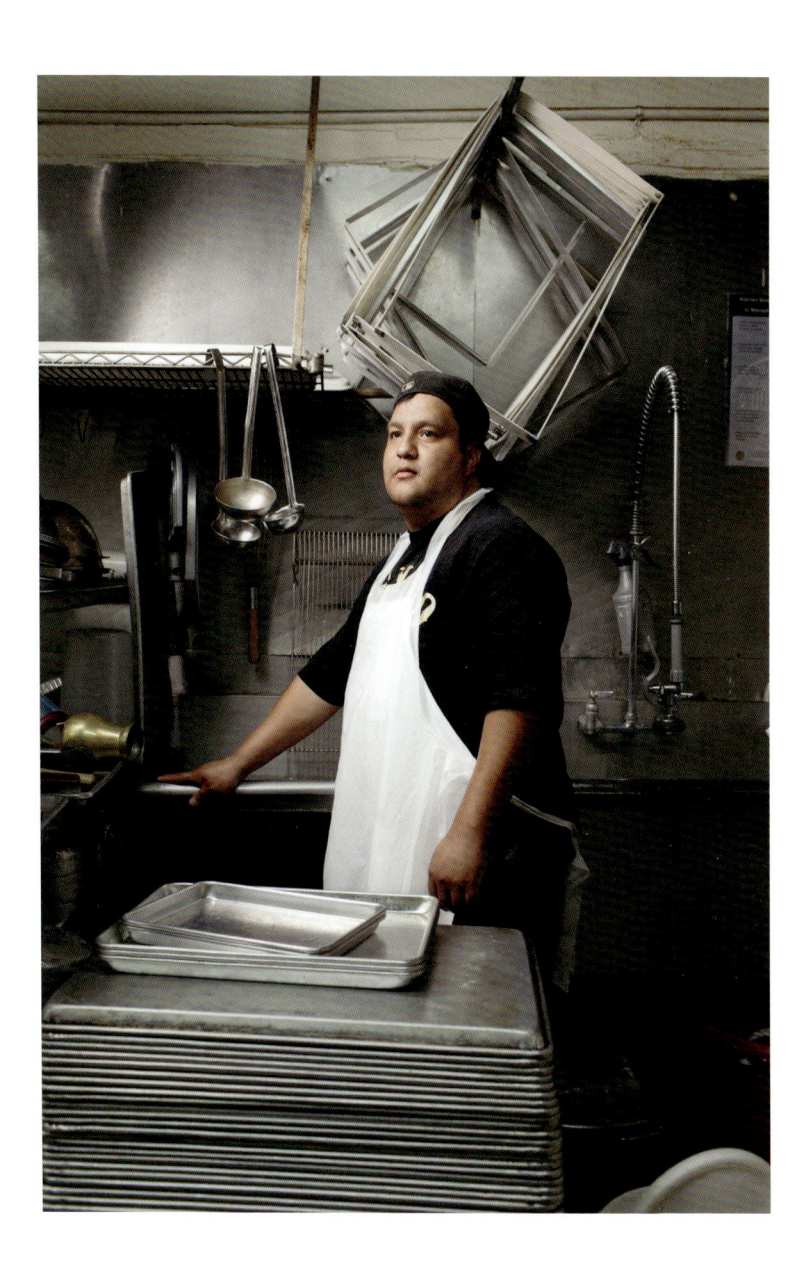

Second Prize

Jesus Sera, Dishwasher

Sam Comen (Los Angeles, California)
Inkjet print, 106.7 × 76.2 cm (42 × 30 in.), 2018
Collection of the artist

Third Prize (tie)

This carefree portrait of teenagers radiates youth, energy, and spunkiness. Hanging out after school on a sunny Wednesday afternoon, they personalize their uniforms of khakis and polo shirts with stylish accessories. A sassy girl with long braids fronts the group. Posing proudly for the camera with her arms crossed, legs anchored in the shape of an A, and a playfully defiant head-tilt, she asserts her presence with a joyful fearlessness. To her left, a girl in profile also looks straight at the camera, although her expression and bouncy curls convey more sweetness than attitude. Most of the boys in the background smile while their friend shows off.

  The group's body language is relaxed yet energetic, and the chromatic counterpoint of the hot pink building and the shades of blue smattered across the picture-plane accentuate this sense of dynamism. These kids are in their element. Richard Greene captured this display of teen spirit while passing through the outskirts of Monroe, Louisiana, on a coast-to-coast road trip. It is part of a series of photographs he is developing on the rural South.

  Greene, who is a trained classical violinist and bluegrass fiddle master, has been passionate about photography since his teenage years. He identifies expression, innovation, technique, and composition as the four pillars of his creative endeavors.

— Taína Caragol

Third Prize (tie)

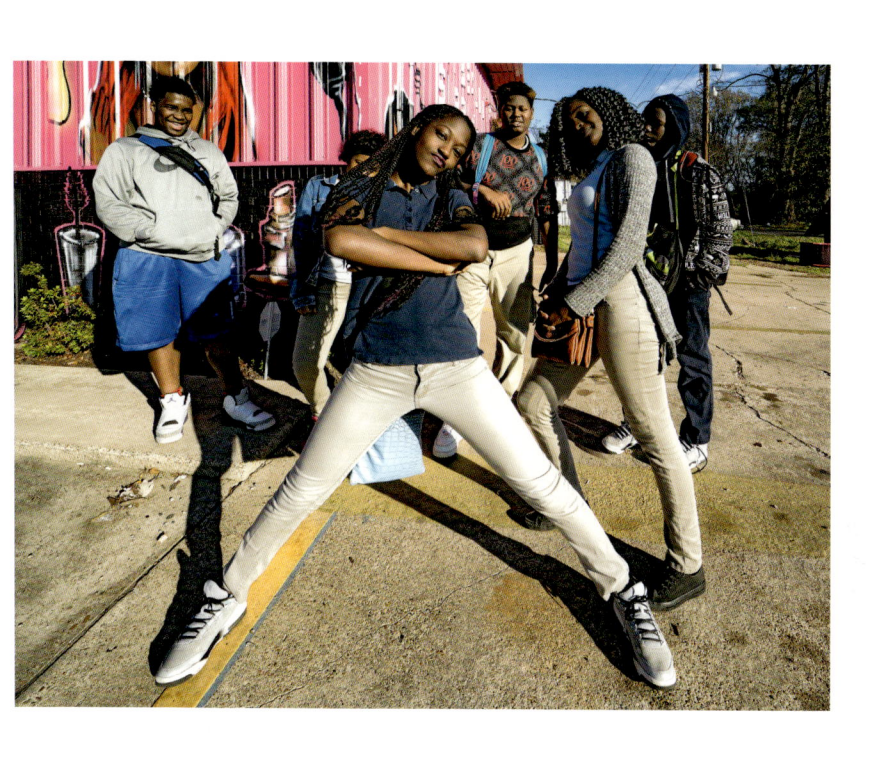

Monroe, LA

Richard Greene (Los Angeles, California)
Inkjet print, 43.2 × 61 cm (17 × 24 in.), 2016
Collection of the artist

Third Prize (tie)

This small-scale portrait by the painter Wayde McIntosh brims with detail. At its center, a seated woman, shown from the torso up, rests her head on the back of her hand. She confronts our gaze through large black-rimmed glasses but nonetheless seems to encourage us to examine her surroundings. Behind her, a golden pothos plant cascades down a packed bookshelf, which prominently displays a copy of *Time* magazine from April 20, 2015, with "Black Lives Matter" on the cover. Hanging on the wall is a photograph of two men standing with their right hands on their hearts. According to McIntosh, "A portrait should not only be a likeness of the sitter. The setting should also help in establishing the sitter's history, personality, and character."

Legacy embodies this kind of portrait. The subject is McIntosh's close friend, the artist Jordan Casteel, who is known for her sensitive and expressive portraits of African American men. Casteel carries on a long tradition of individuals advocating for social justice. Her grandfather, the civil rights leader Whitney Young Jr., served as the Executive Director of the National Urban League and helped organize the 1963 March on Washington for Jobs and Freedom. The black-and-white photograph pictures him next to Martin Luther King Jr., who delivered his legendary speech, "I Have a Dream," at that event. McIntosh juxtaposes the historical photograph with a recent copy of *Time* to imply that while times have changed, social issues remain the same.

The red, black, and green flag is a replica of the iconic *African American Flag* (1990), created by the artist David Hammons. One edition of Hammons's flag hangs at the entrance of the Studio Museum in Harlem, which has promoted artists of African descent, including Casteel, who participated in the museum's prestigious artist-in-residence program. Casteel's vitality and her future legacy are symbolized by the pothos, which can thrive in harsh environments. Nothing is in excess in this portrait, where each object in some way connects with the sitter.

— Taína Caragol

Third Prize (tie)

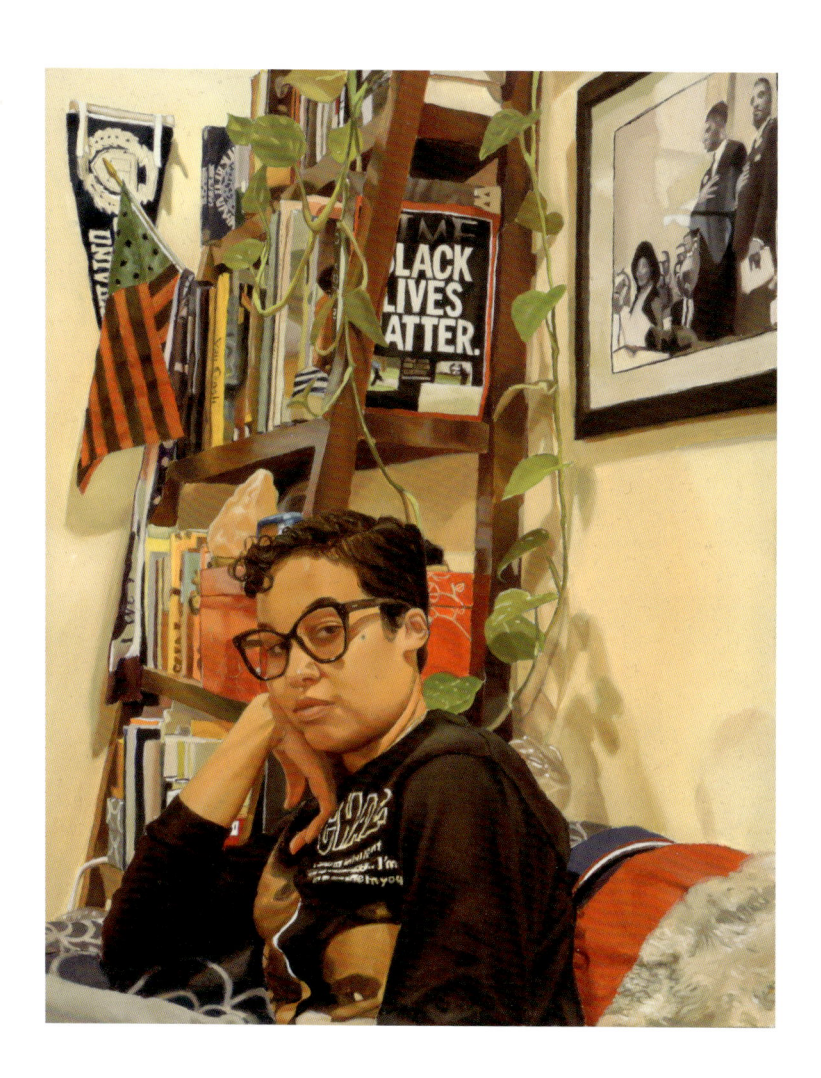

Legacy

Wayde McIntosh (Brooklyn, New York)
Oil on Dibond, 25.4 × 20.3 cm (10 × 8 in.), 2017
Collection of the artist

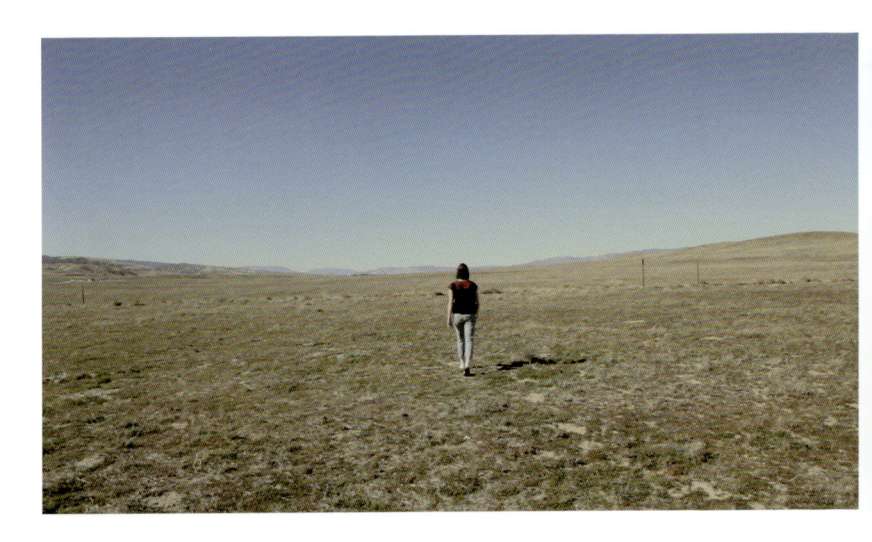

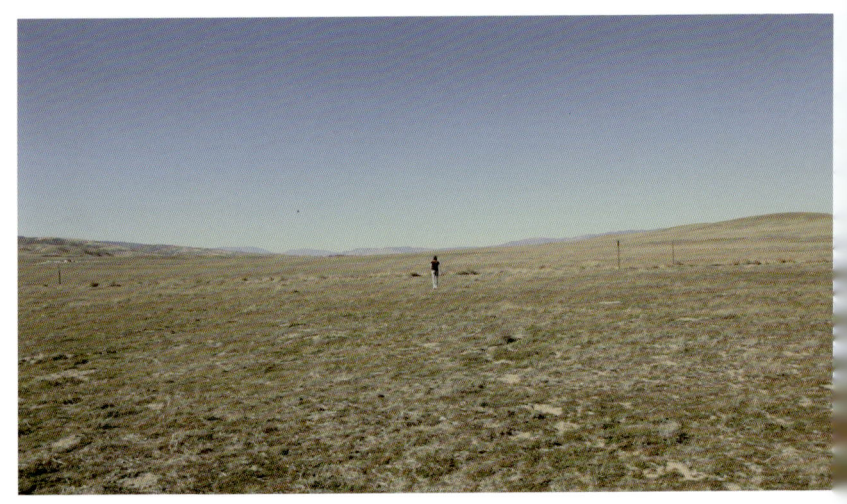

Commended

Self-Portrait

Natalia Garcia Clark (Los Angeles, California, and Mexico City)
HD video (5:59 min.), 2017
Collection of the artist

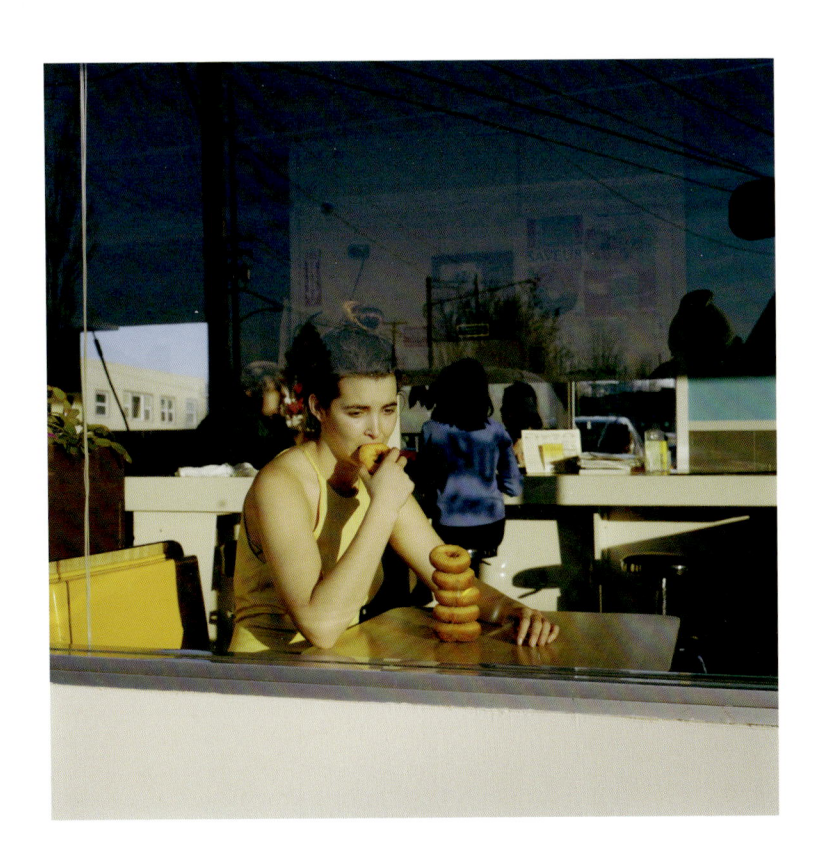

Commended

Secrets

Lauren Hare (Portland, Oregon)
Inkjet print, 61 × 61 cm (24 × 24 in.), 2017
Collection of the artist

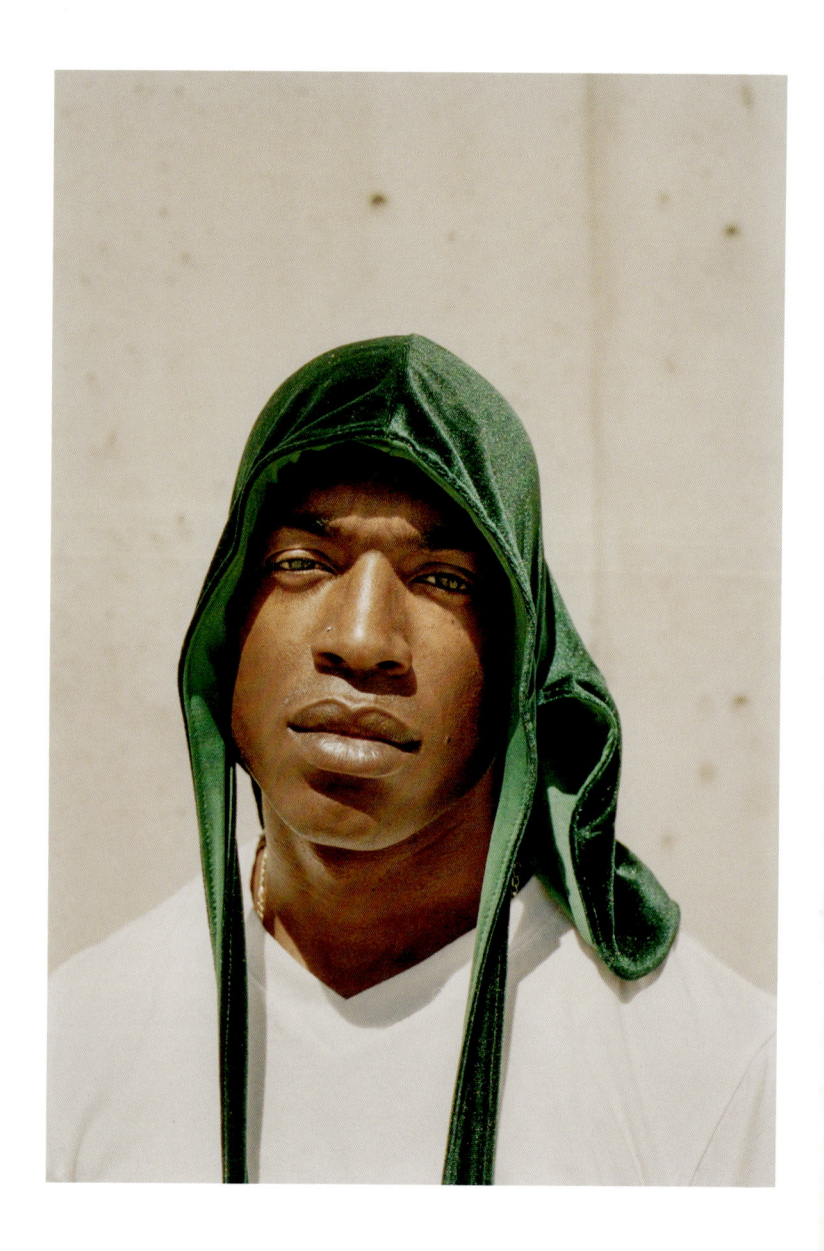

Commended

Black Virgin Mary

Adrian Octavius Walker (Oakland, California)
Inkjet print, 99.7 × 67 cm (39 ¼ × 26 ⅜ in.), 2018
Collection of the artist

Outwin Boochever Portrait Competition Finalists of 2019

in alphabetical order

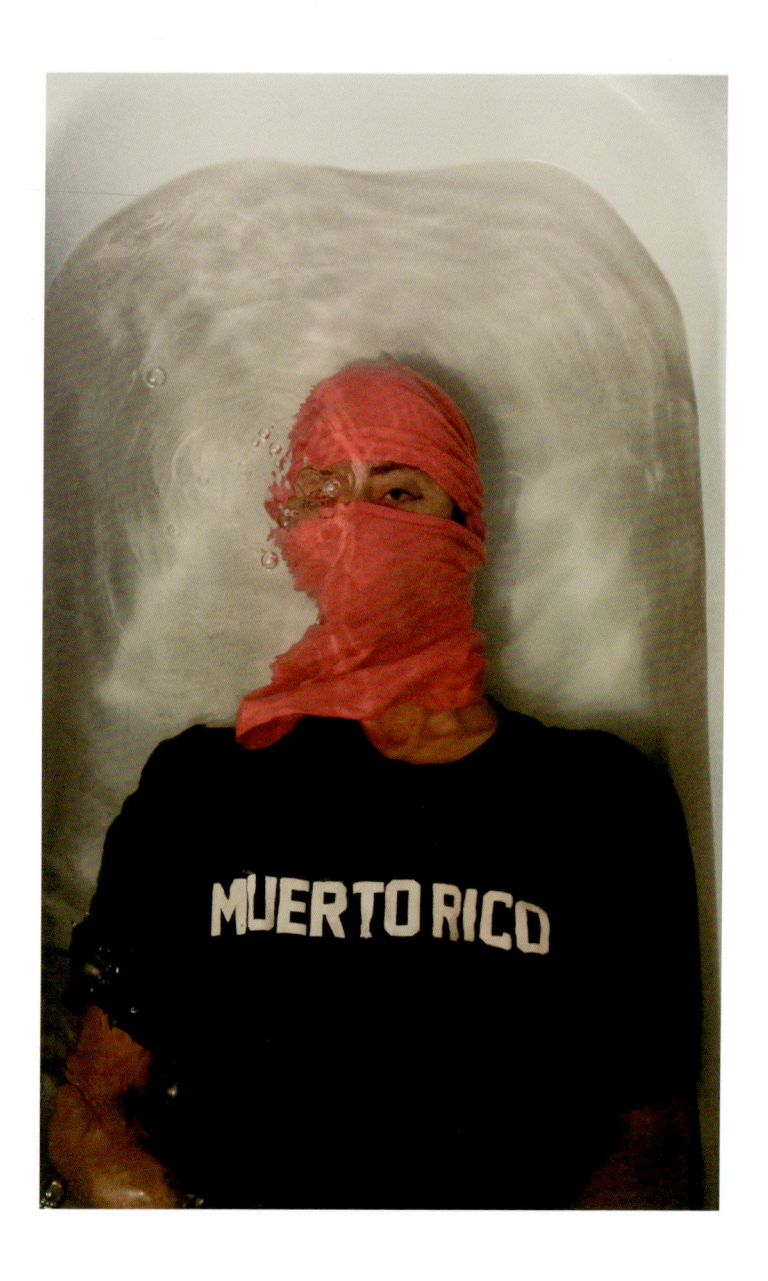

Muerto Rico (from "Puerto Ricans Underwater / Los Ahogados" series)

ADÁL (Santurce, Puerto Rico)
Inkjet print, 128.3 × 81.3 cm (50½ × 32 in.), 2017
Collection of the artist

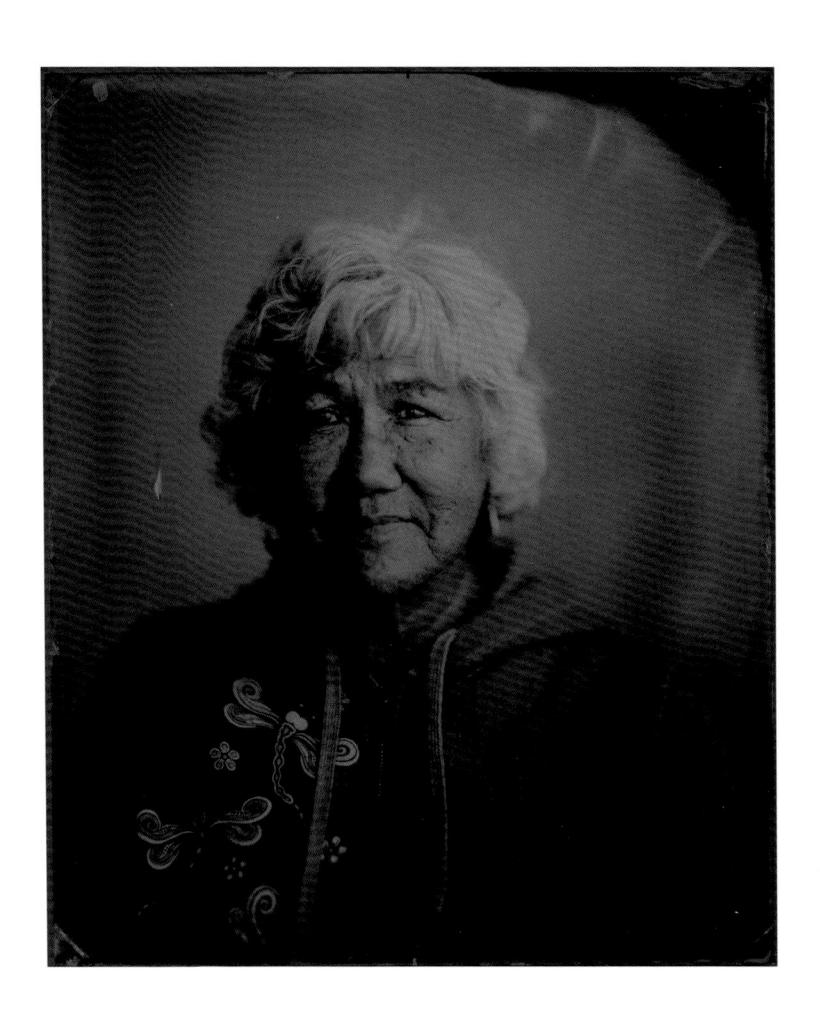

Florence Pestrikoff,
One of the Remaining Speakers of Alutiiq

Paul Adams (Lindon, Utah) and Jordan Layton (Los Angeles, California)
Wet-collodion tintype, 61 × 50.8 cm (24 × 20 in.), 2017
Collection of the artists

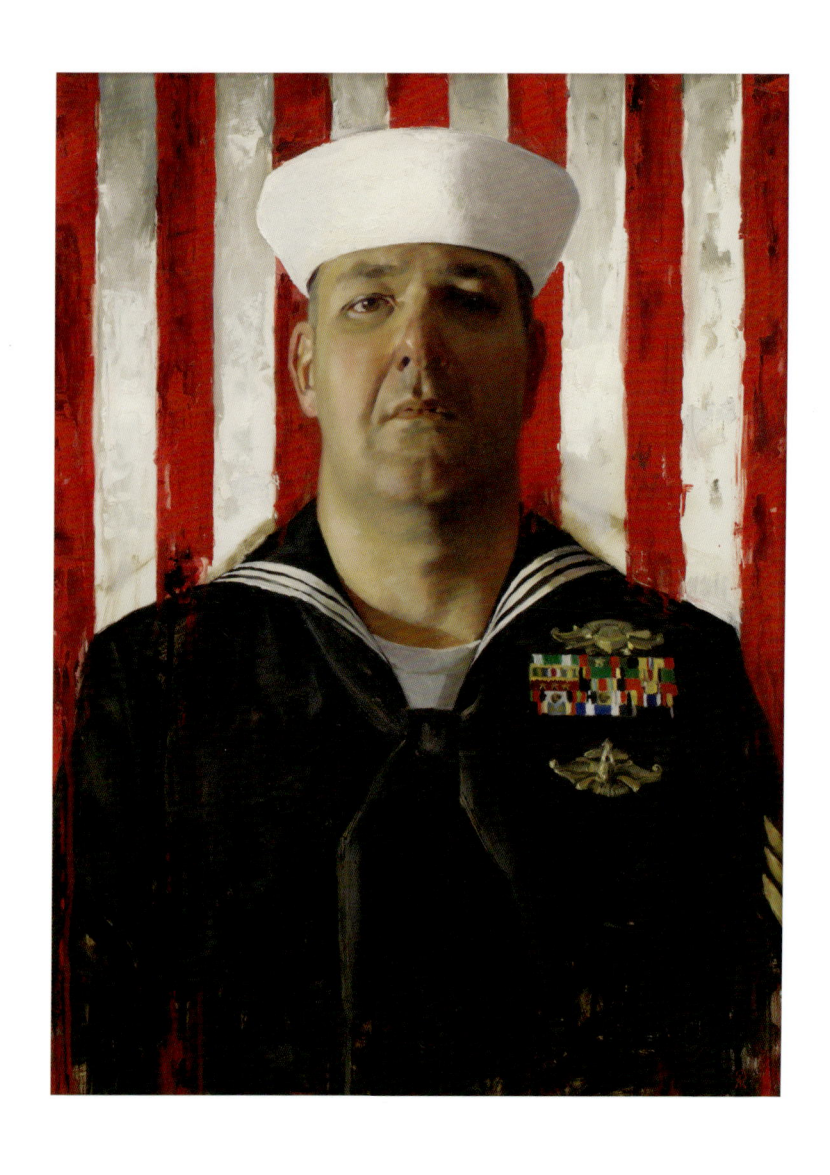

Hidden Wounds

Luis Álvarez Roure (Hasbrouck Heights, New Jersey)
Oil on board, 59.4 × 44.5 cm (23 3/8 × 17 1/2 in.), 2017
Collection of the artist

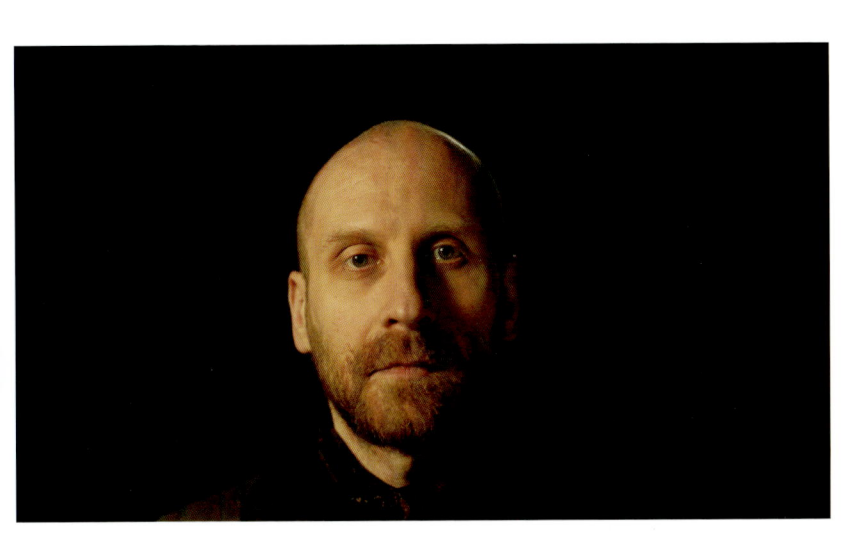

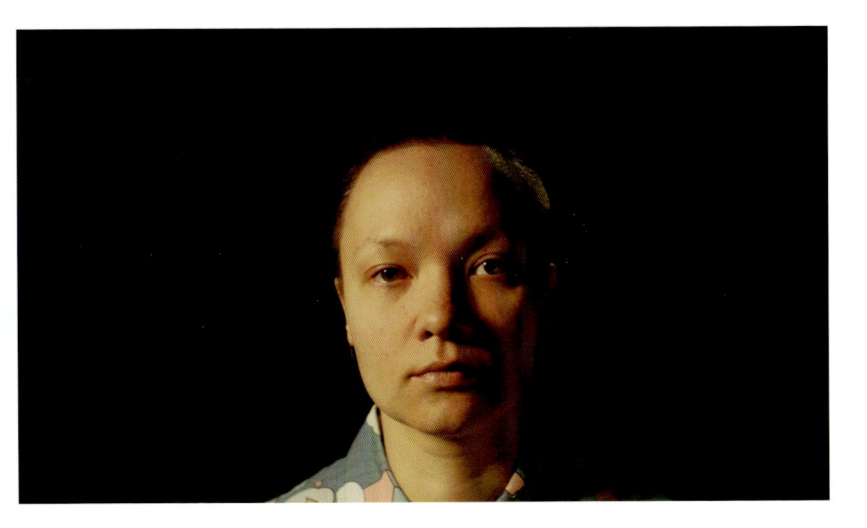

Night Watch

Shimon Attie (New York, New York)
HD video (9:48 min.), 2018
Collection of the artist and Jack Shainman Gallery, New York
Originally commissioned and produced by More Art, NYC

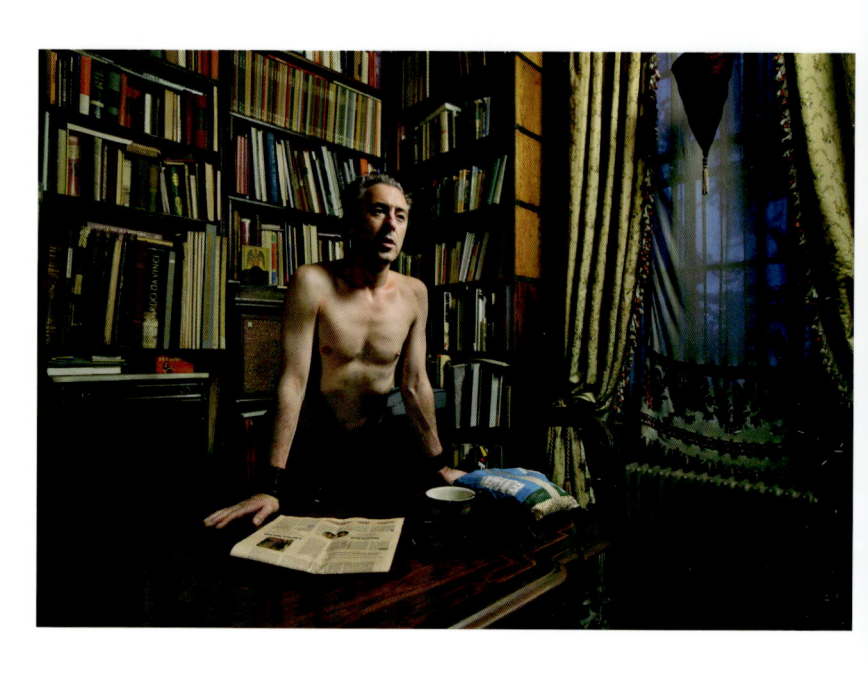

Alan Cumming

Tom Atwood (New York, New York)
Inkjet print, 45.1 × 65.4 cm (17 ¾ × 25 ¾ in.), 2017
Collection of the artist

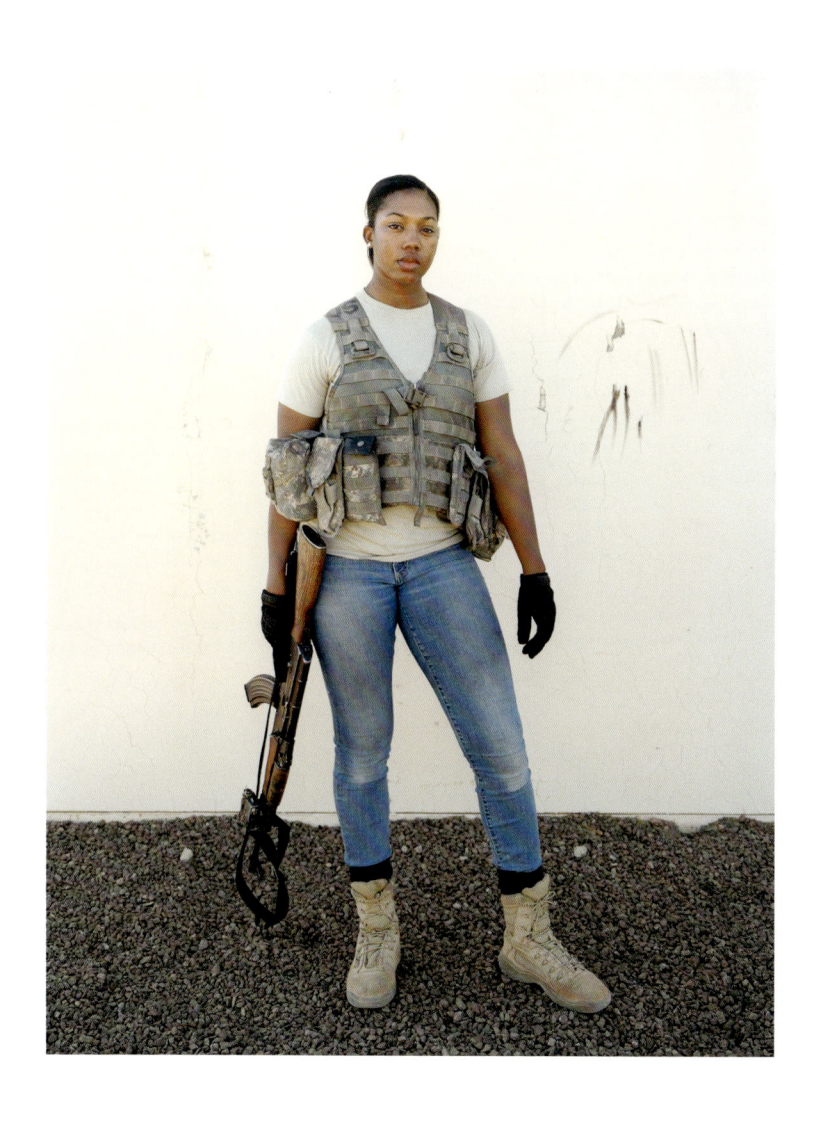

Lead Insurgent Sergeant Ariel Combs

Claire Beckett (Swampscott, Massachusetts)
Inkjet print, 100.3 × 79.7 cm (39½ × 31⅜ in.), 2017
Collection of the artist

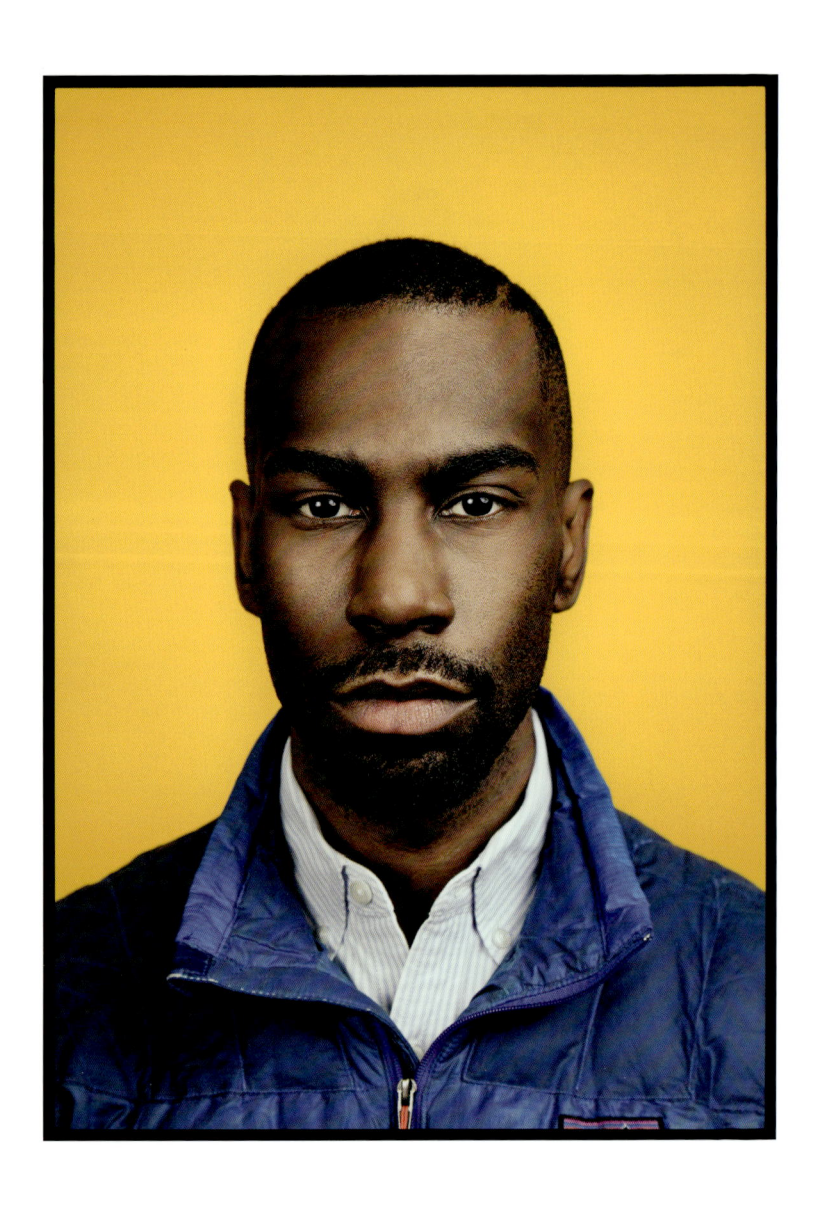

DeRay Mckesson

Quinn Russell Brown (Seattle, Washington)
Inkjet print, 101.6 × 71.1 cm (40 × 28 in.), 2018
Collection of the artist, courtesy of the University of Washington

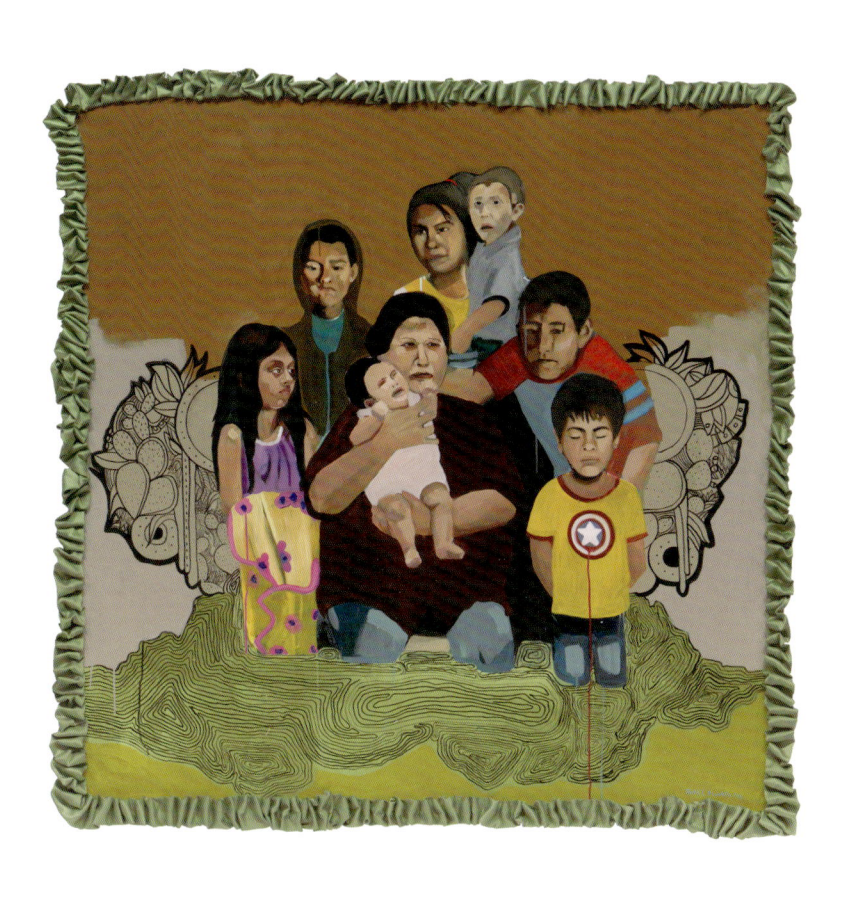

Desaparecidos en el Río Bravo (Disappeared in the Río Bravo)

Ruth Leonela Buentello (San Antonio, Texas)
Acrylic paint on canvas with fabric, 152.4 × 152.7 cm (60 × 60 1/8 in.), 2018
Collection of the artist

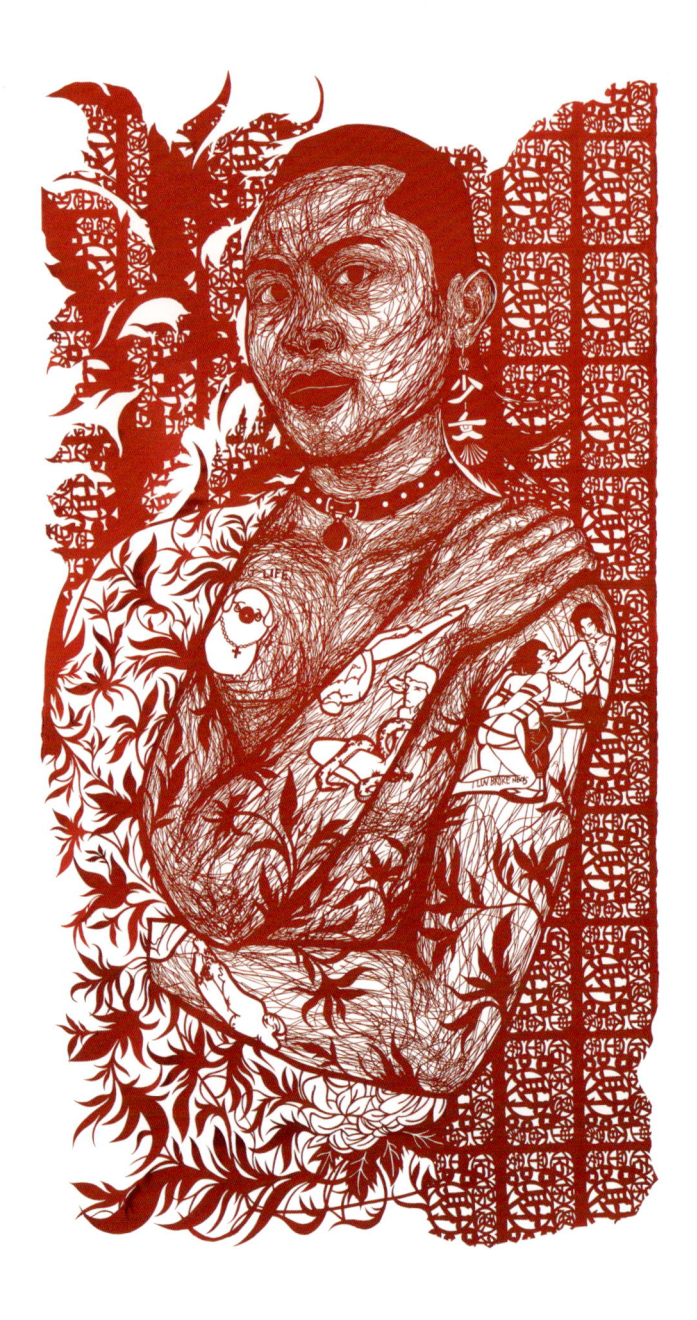

Vanguard

Antonius-Tin Bui (Houston, Texas)
Hand-cut paper, 198.1 × 106.7 cm (78 × 42 in.), 2018
Collection of the artist

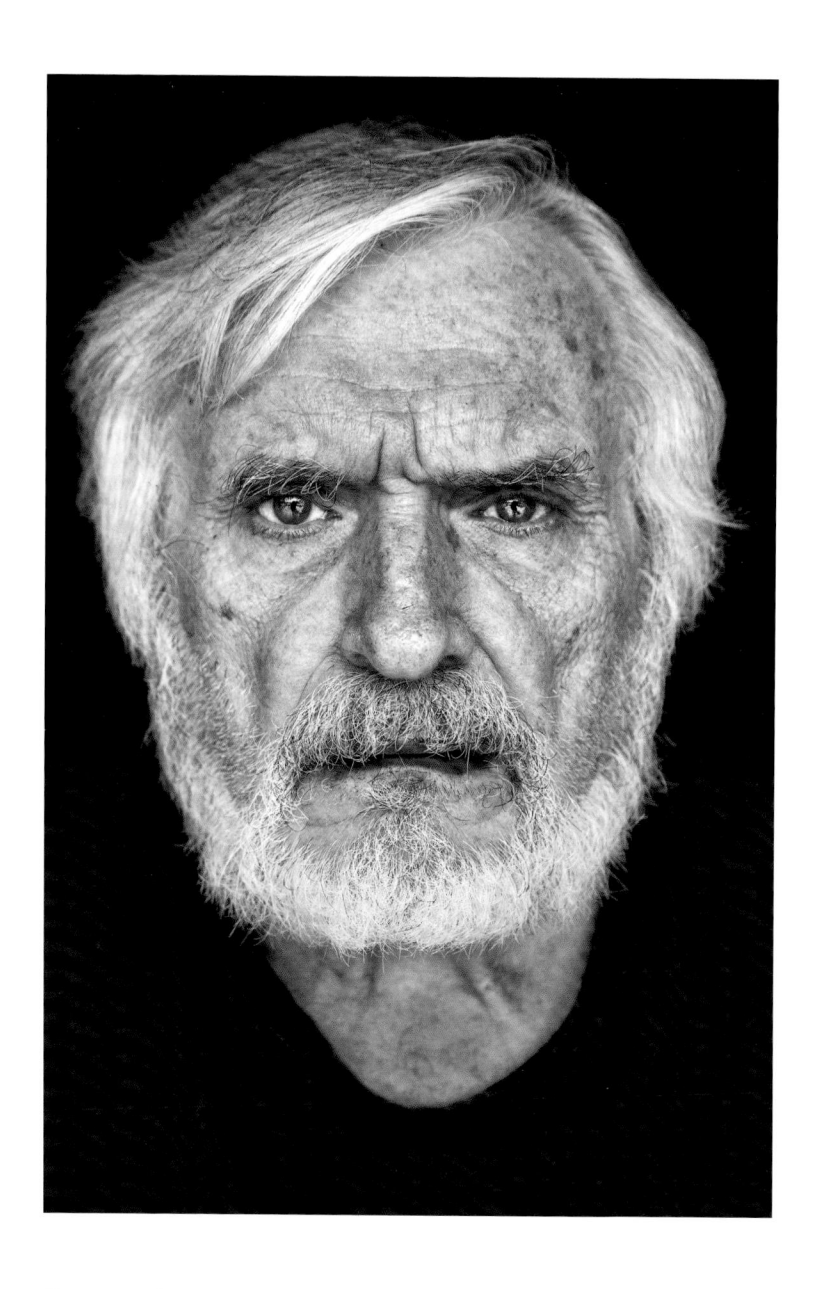

George, b. 1943
(from "Landscapes of a Lifetime" series)

Mike Byrnside (San Antonio, Texas)
Inkjet print, 114.3 × 76.2 cm (45 × 30 in.), 2017
Collection of the artist

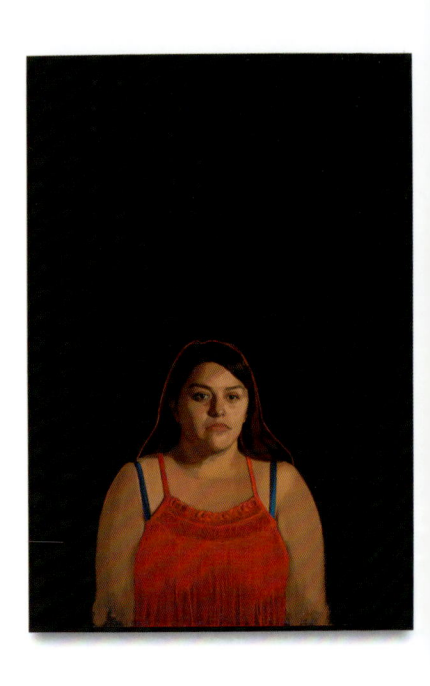

Unaccompanied

Kate Capshaw (New York, New York)
Oil on canvas, each 162.6 × 111.8 cm (64 × 44 in.), 2017
Collection of the artist

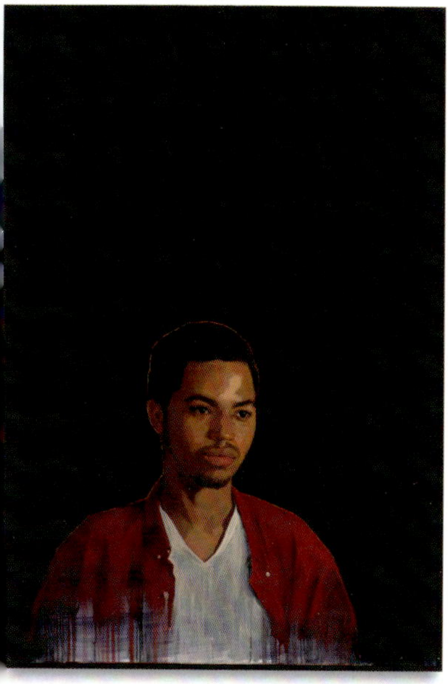

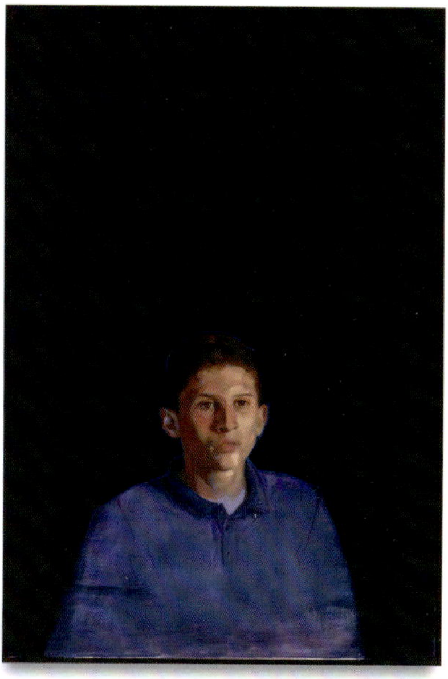

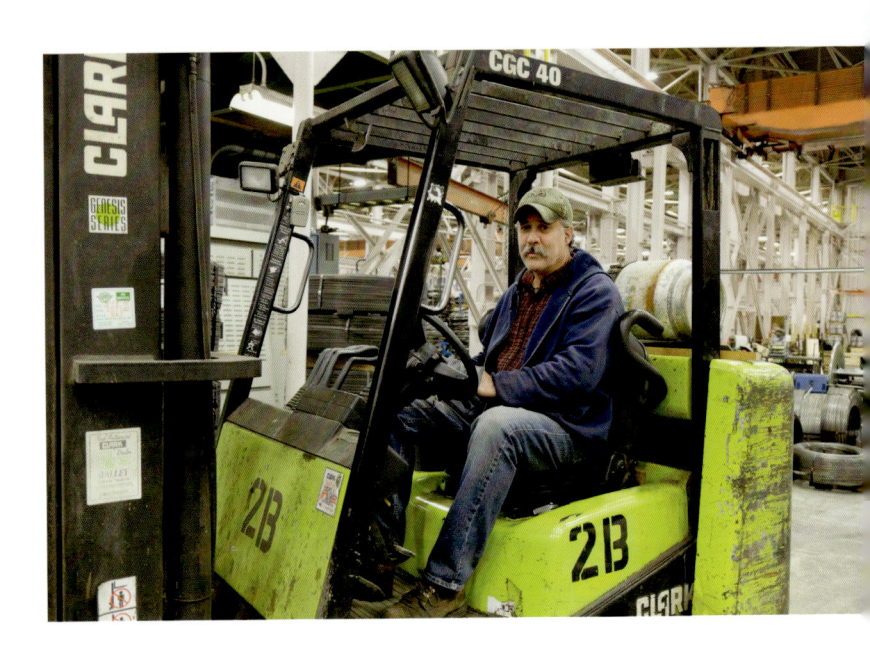

Dad on the Towmotor

Daniel Centofanti (Stevenson Ranch, California)
Inkjet print, 50.8 × 76.2 cm (20 × 30 in.), 2018
Collection of the artist

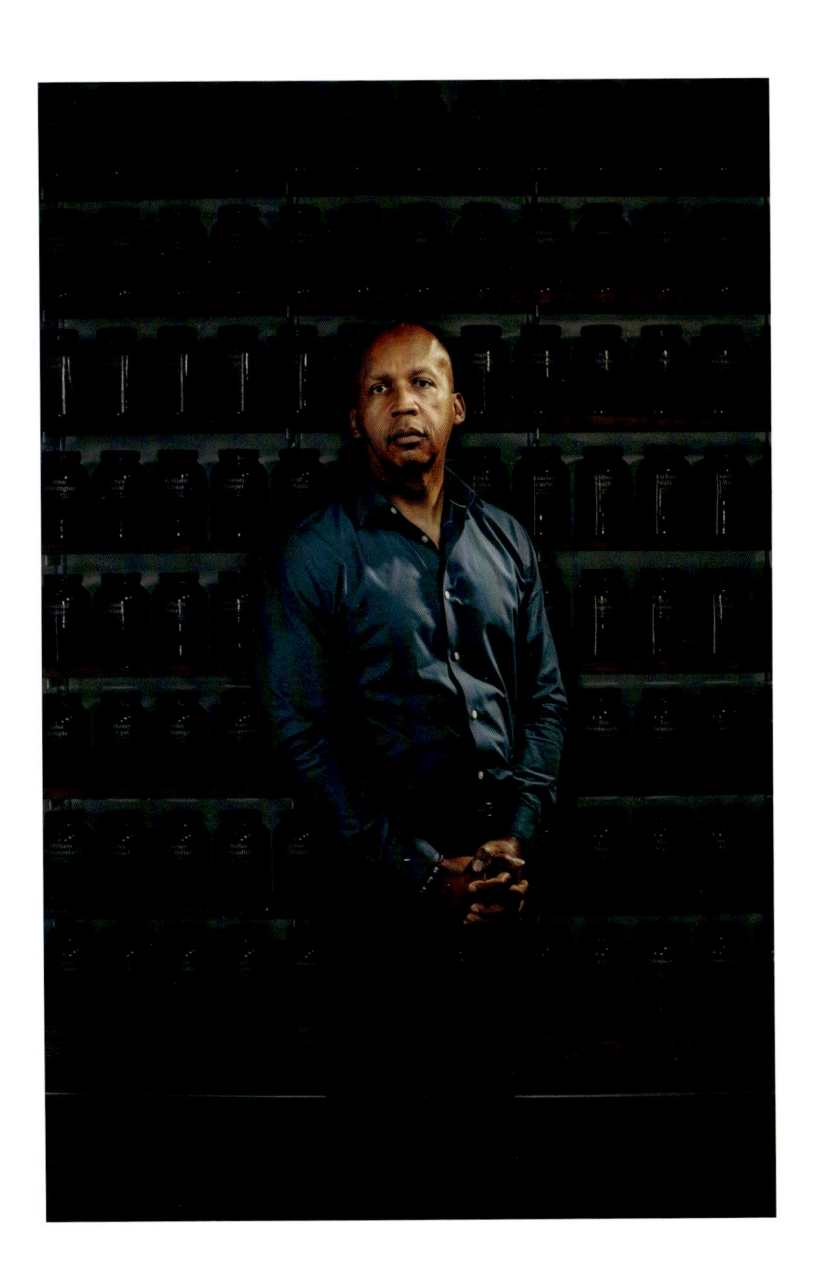

Bryan Stevenson

Joshua Cogan (Washington, D.C.)
Inkjet print, 99.1 × 66 cm (39 × 26 in.), 2018
Collection of the artist

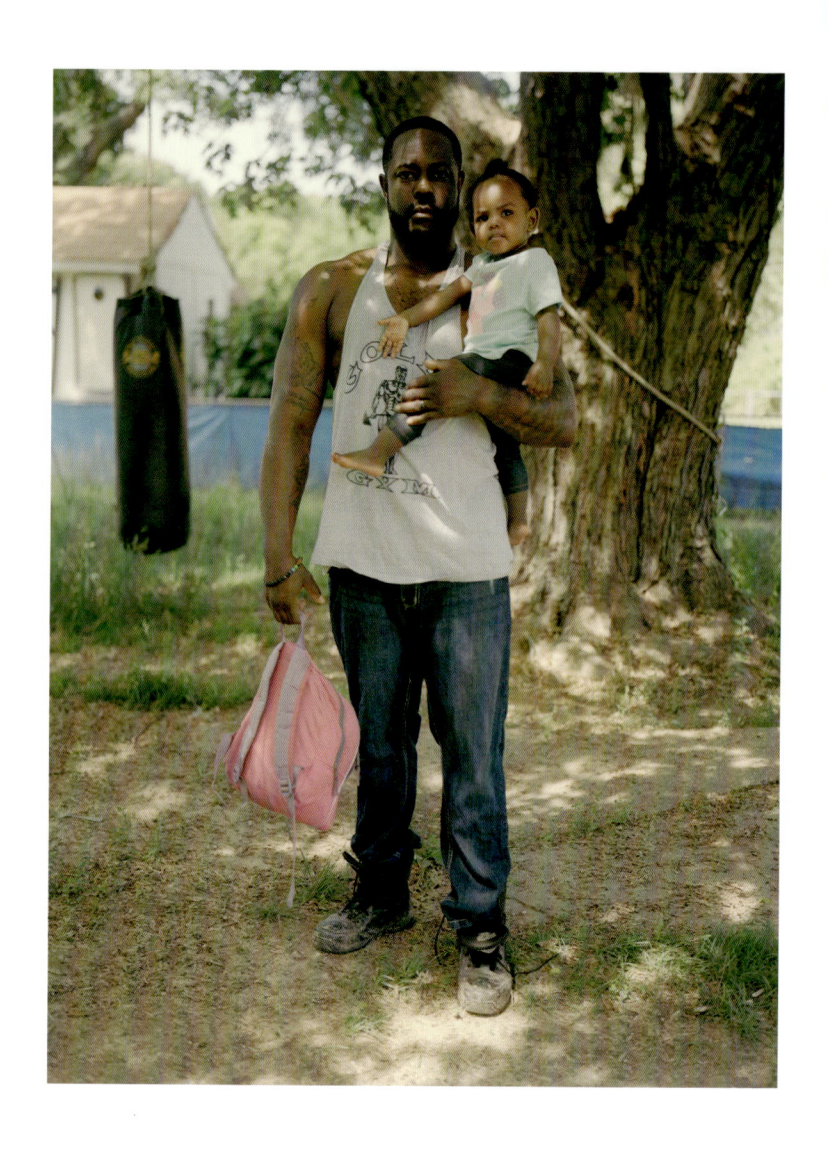

Fatherhood 2

Larry W. Cook Jr. (Washington, D.C.)
Inkjet print, 100.5 × 74.9 cm (39 9/16 × 29 1/2 in.), 2018
Collection of the artist

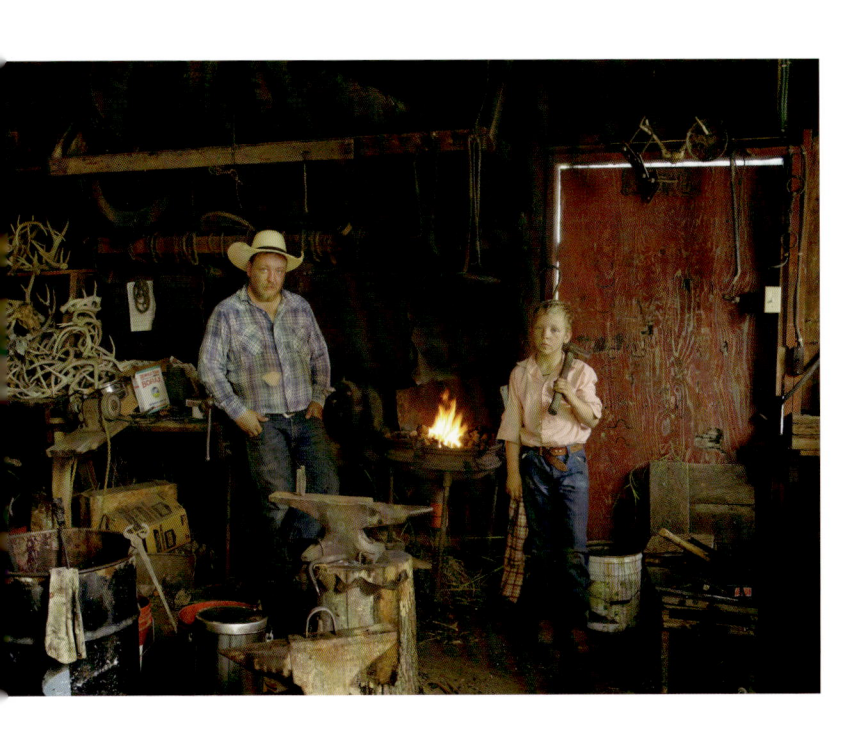

Chance and Gus Forging Spurs

Carl Corey (River Falls, Wisconsin)
Inkjet print, 56 × 74.6 cm (22 1/16 × 29 3/8 in.), 2016
Collection of the artist

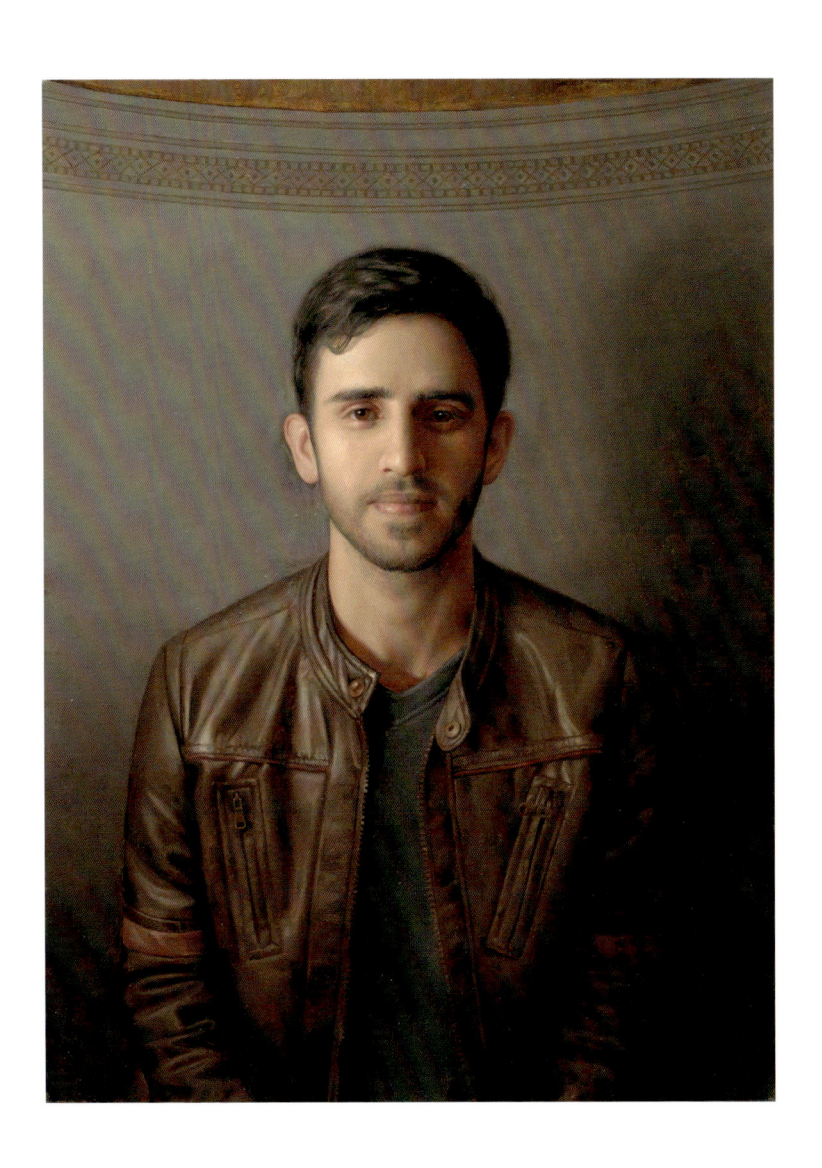

Ajmal, Refugee from Afghanistan

Carla Crawford (Petaluma, California)
Oil on linen, 61 × 45.4 cm (24 × 17⅞ in.), 2016
Collection of the artist

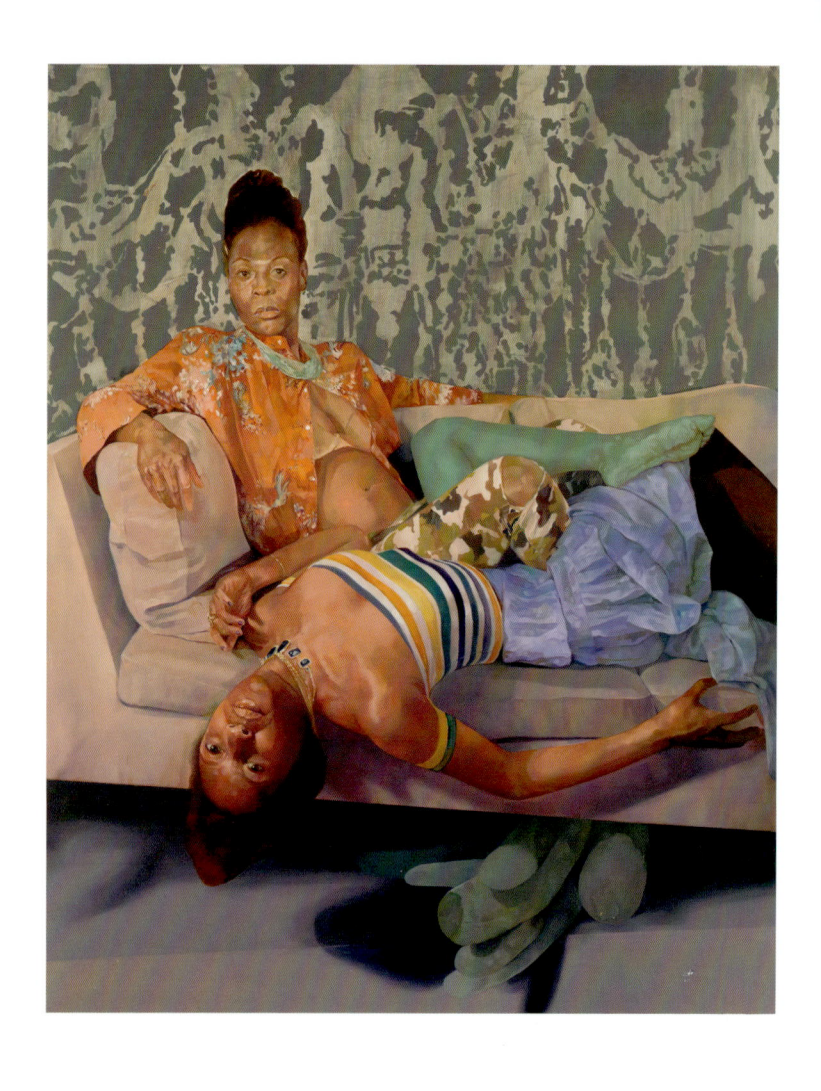

theboysdon'tplaynicewithanyone,
portrait of april and june

David Antonio Cruz (Brooklyn, New York, and Boston, Massachusetts)
Oil and latex on wood, 152.1 × 121.9 cm (59 7/8 × 48 in.), 2018
Collection of the artist

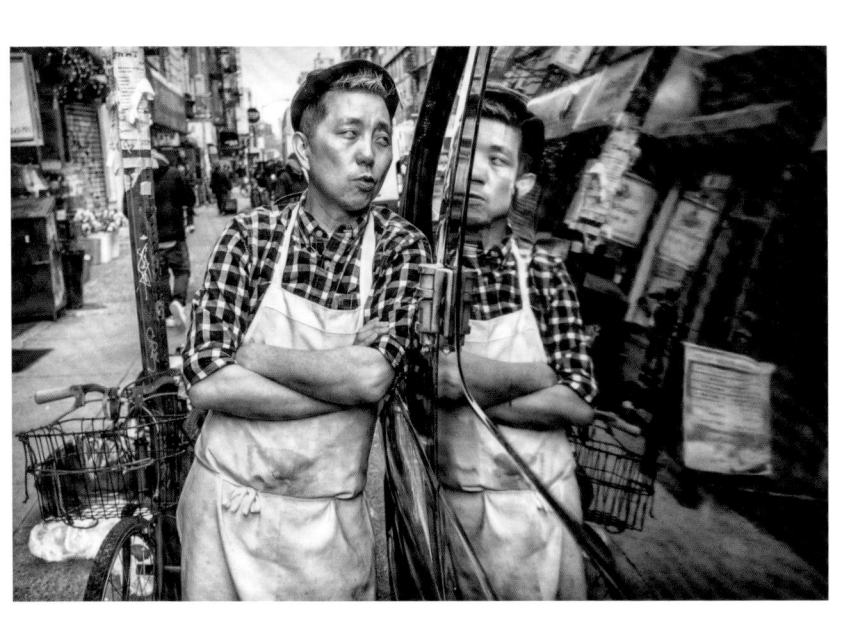

Chinatown, New York City

Ronald Diamond (Brooklyn, New York)
Inkjet print, 24.1 × 36.8 cm (9½ × 14½ in.), 2018
Collection of the artist

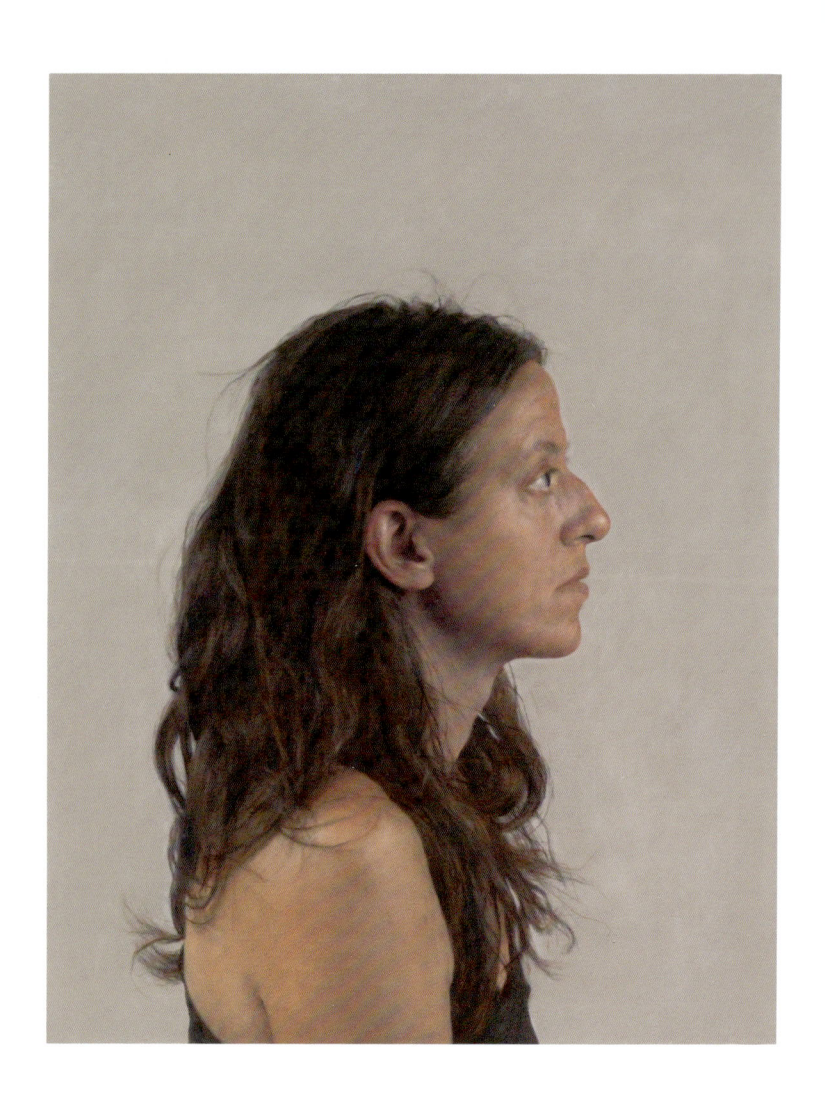

TZ in Profile

Jenny Dubnau (Queens, New York)
Oil on canvas, 116.2 × 91.4 cm (45¾ × 36 in.), 2016
Collection of the artist

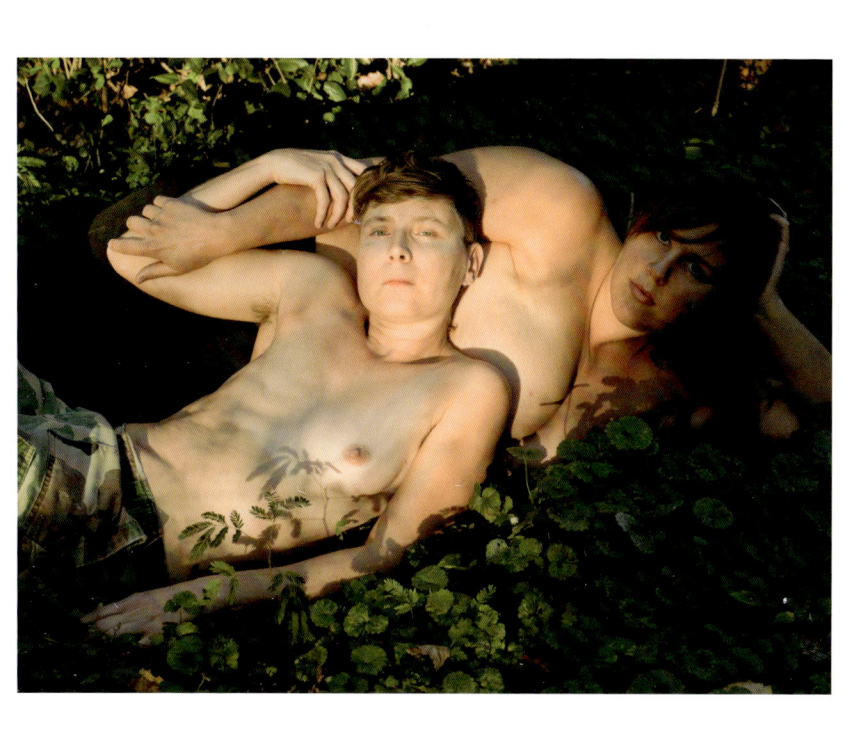

Jamie and Ann

Jess T. Dugan (St. Louis, Missouri)
Inkjet print, 74.9 × 100.3 cm (29½ × 39½ in.), 2016
Collection of the artist, courtesy of the Catherine Edelman Gallery, Chicago

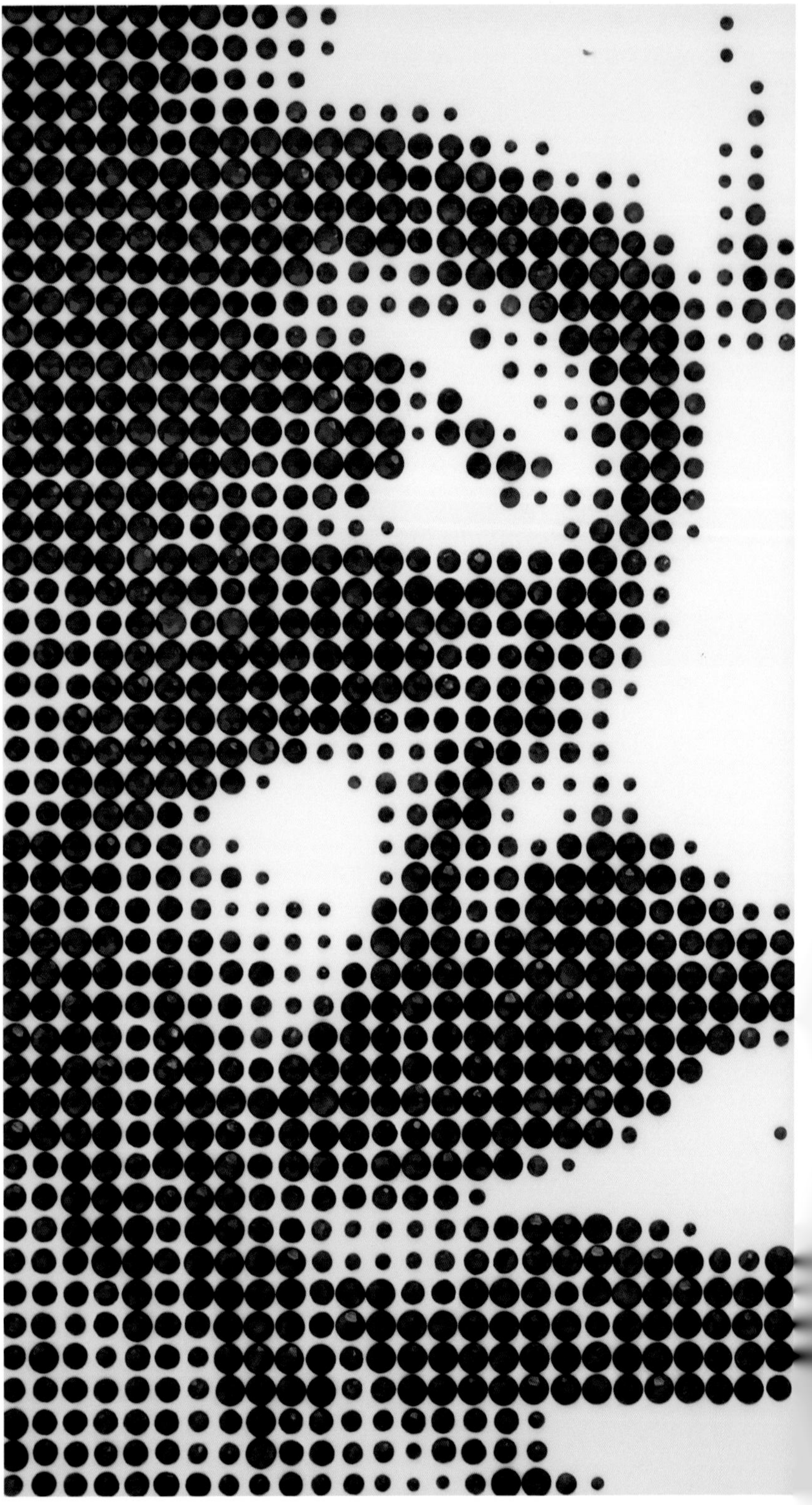

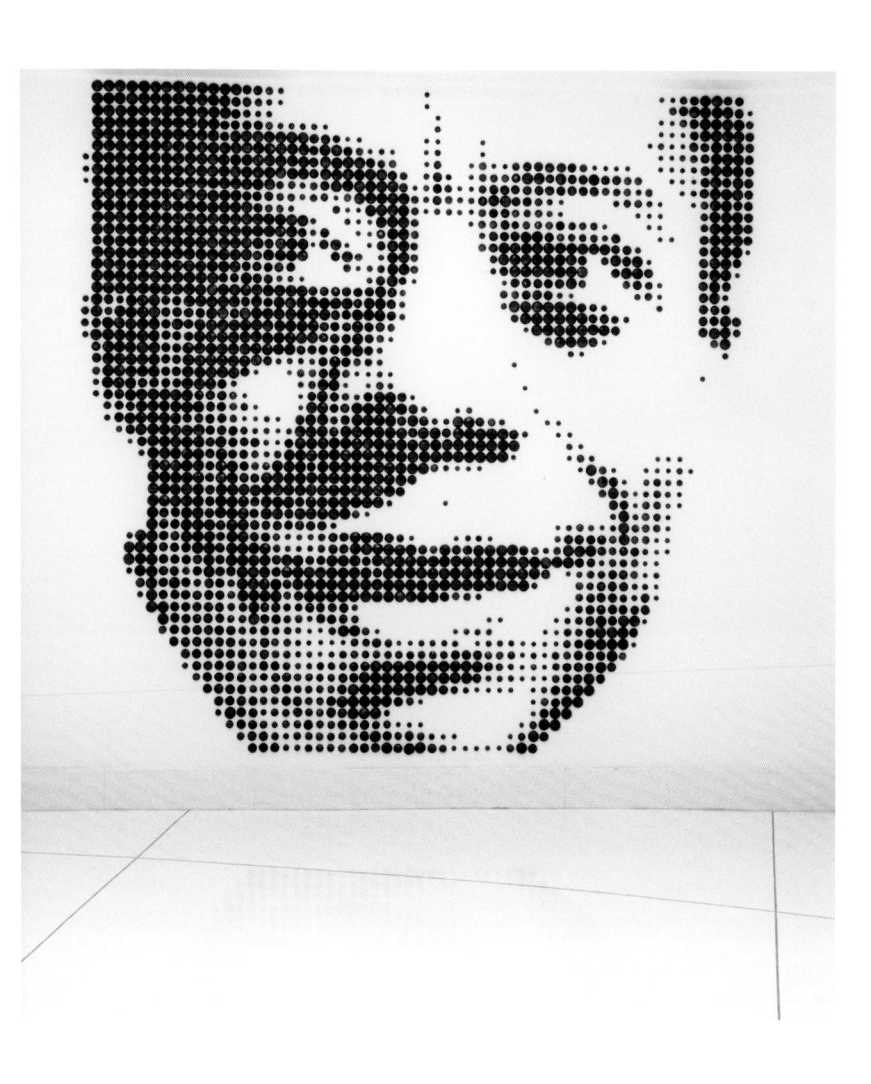

James Baldwin

Nekisha Durrett (Washington, D.C.)
Polymer clay, 213.4 × 213.4 × 6.4 cm (84 × 84 × 2½ in.), 2018
Collection of the artist

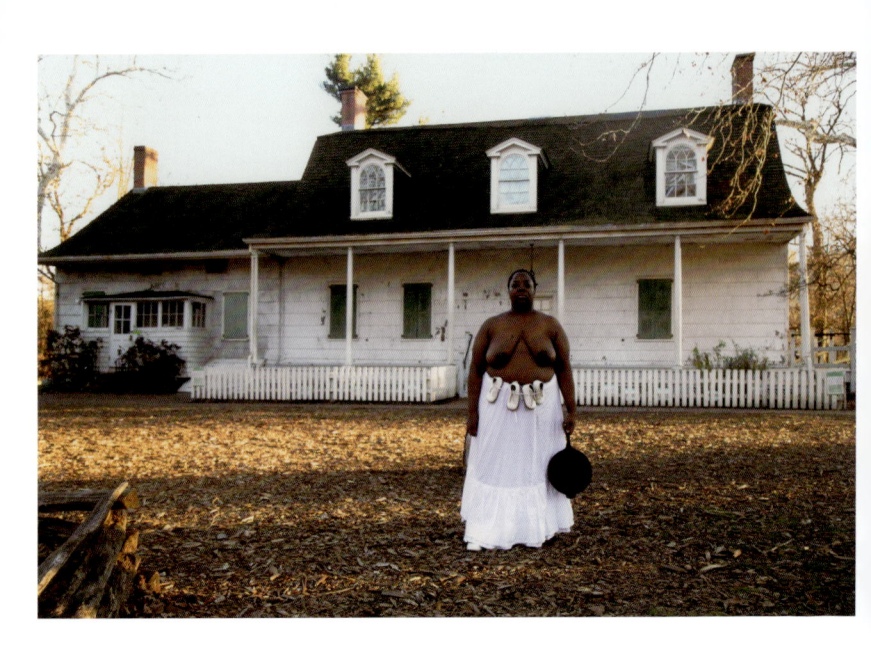

Isabelle, Lefferts House, Brooklyn (Self-Portrait)

Nona Faustine (Brooklyn, New York)
Inkjet print, 67.6 × 101.6 cm (26 5/8 × 40 in.), 2016
Collection of the artist

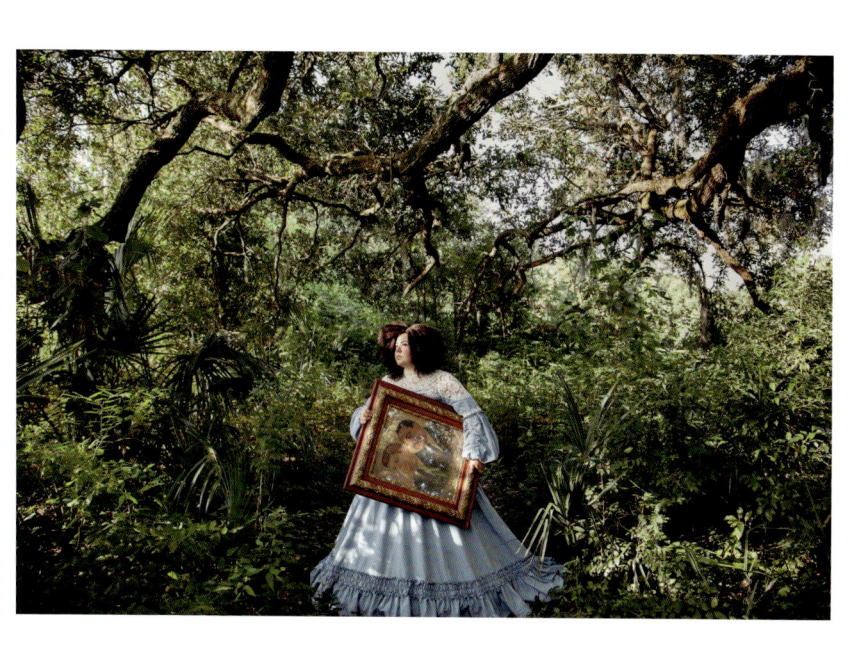

Trailblazer (A Dream Deferred)

Genevieve Gaignard (Los Angeles, California)
Inkjet print, 101.6 × 152.4 cm (40 × 60 in.), 2017
Collection of the artist, courtesy of Vielmetter Los Angeles

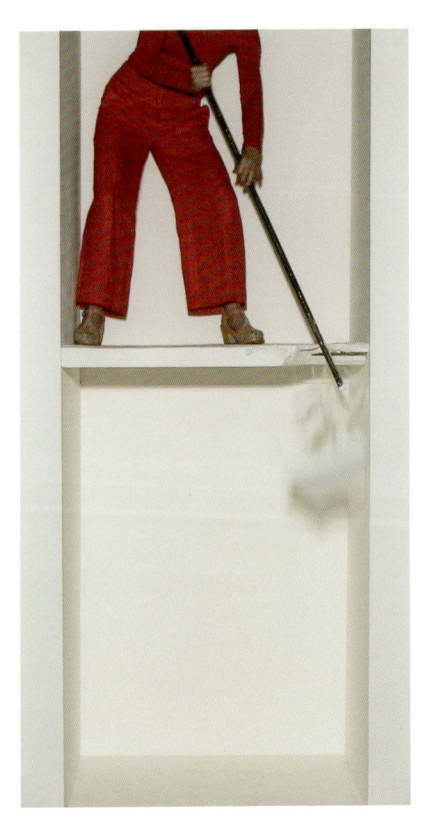

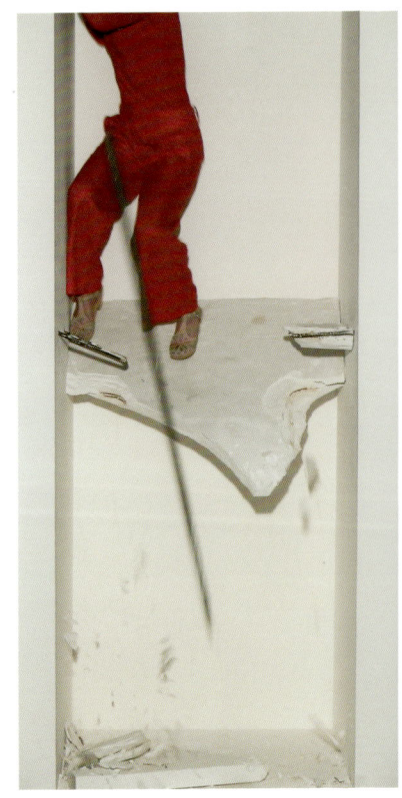

Just Below

Anna Garner (Los Angeles, California)
HD video (4:12 min.), 2016
Collection of the artist

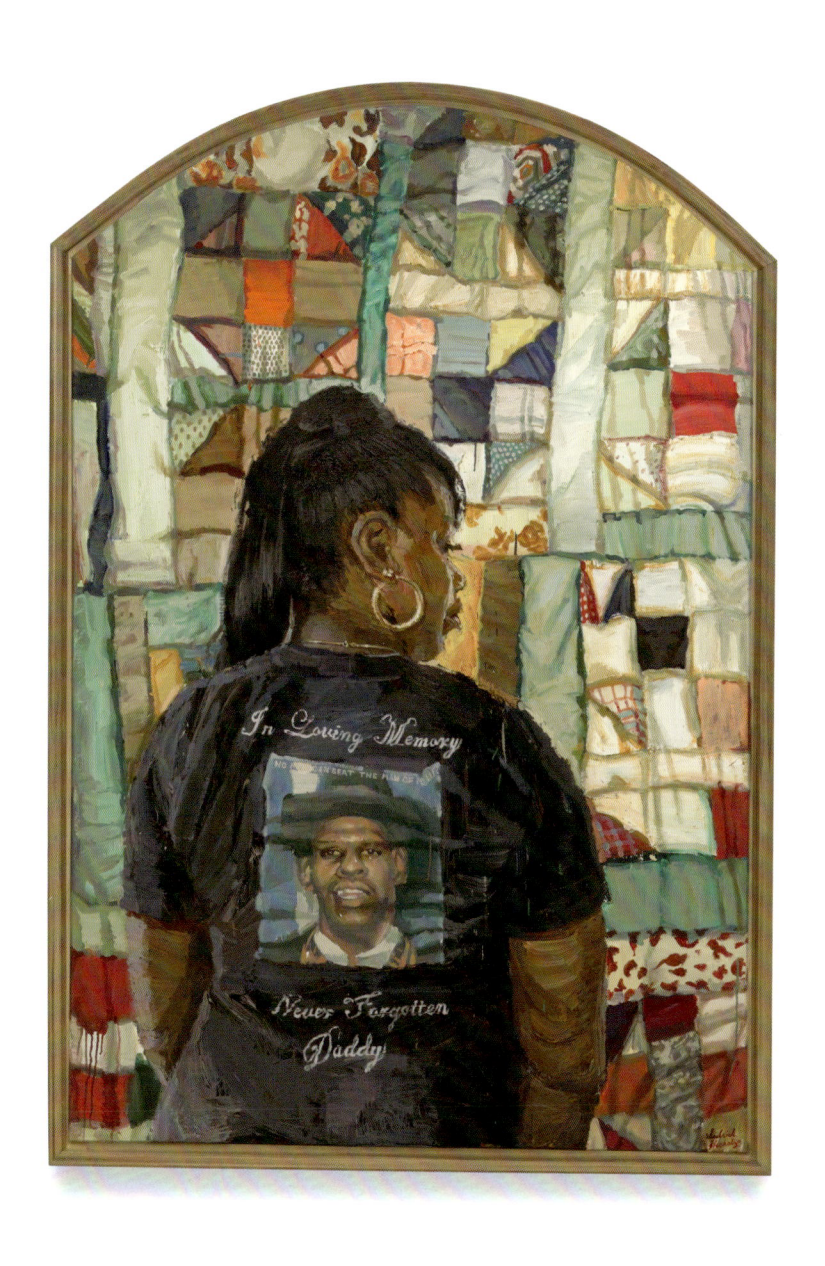

Our Lamentations: Never Forgotten Daddy

Sedrick Huckaby (Benbrook, Texas)
Oil on canvas, 180 × 121.9 cm (70 7/8 × 48 in.), 2018
Collection of the artist

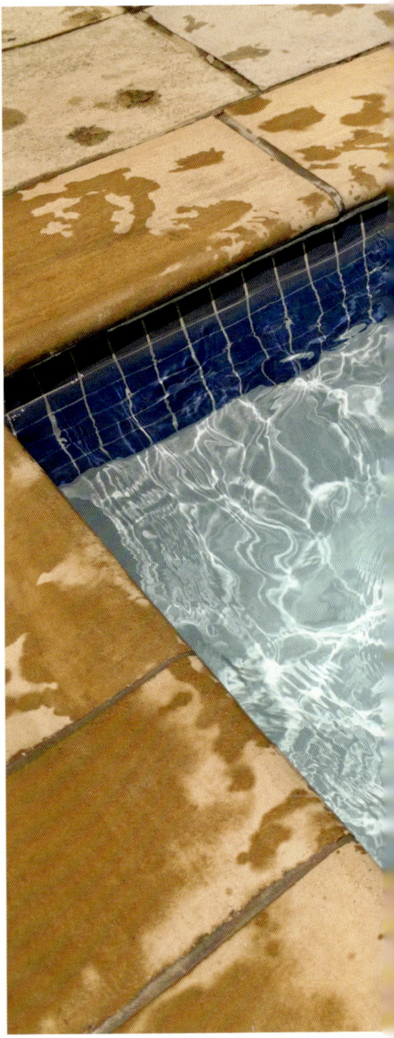

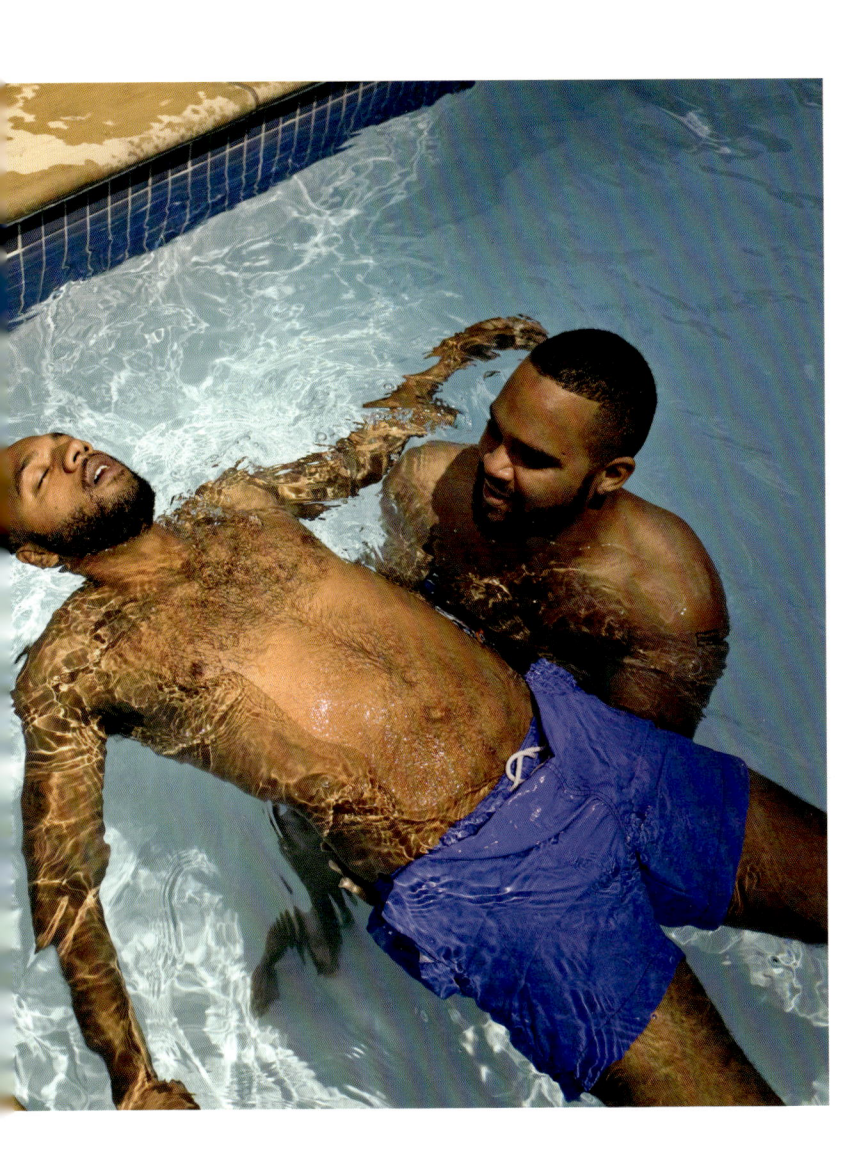

Brendan and Tyrice

Zun Lee (Bronx, New York)
Inkjet print, 76.2 × 101 cm (30 × 39¾ in.), 2016
Collection of the artist

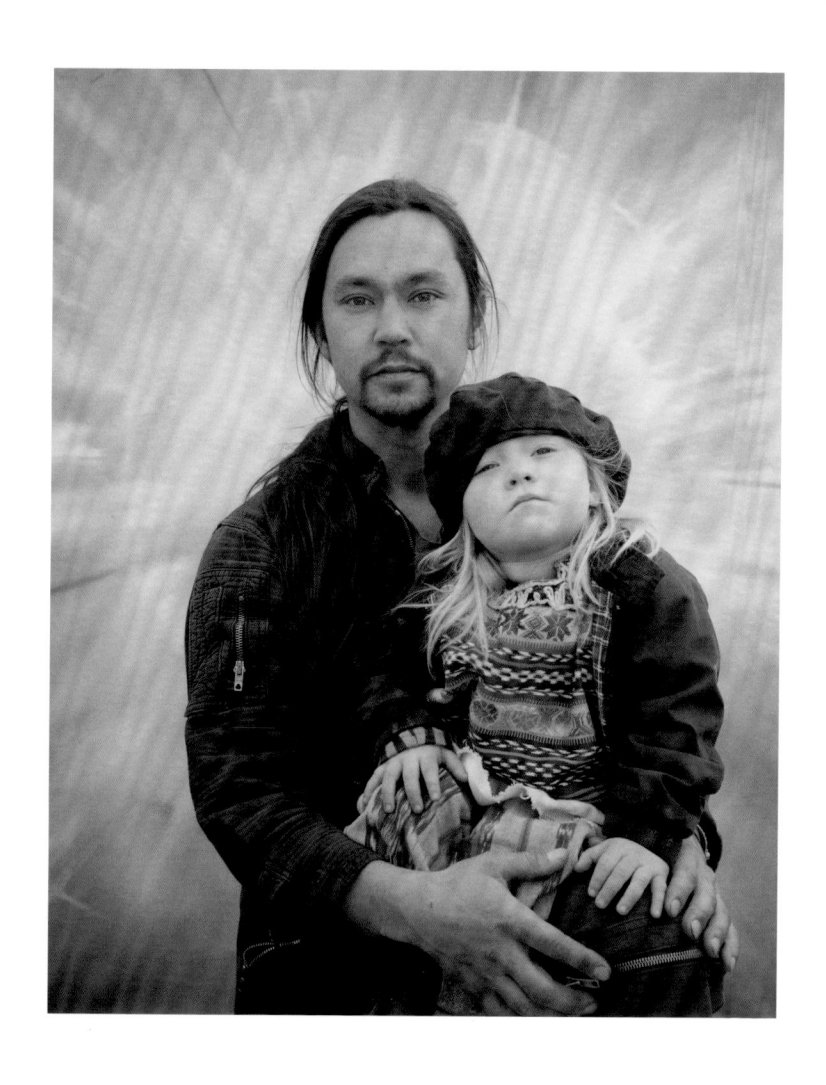

Glenn & Jerusha (from "Deadheads in America Then & Now" series)

William Lemke (Waukesha, Wisconsin)
Inkjet prints, 48.9 × 39.2 cm (19 ¼ × 15 7/16), 1988 and 2018 (printed 2018)
Collection of the artist

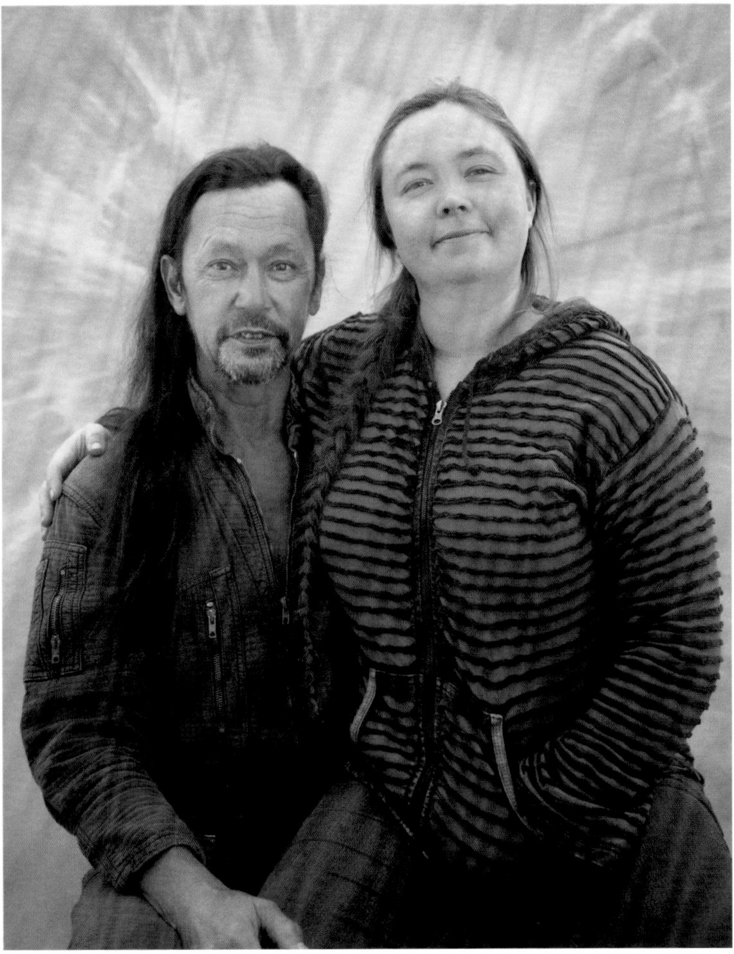

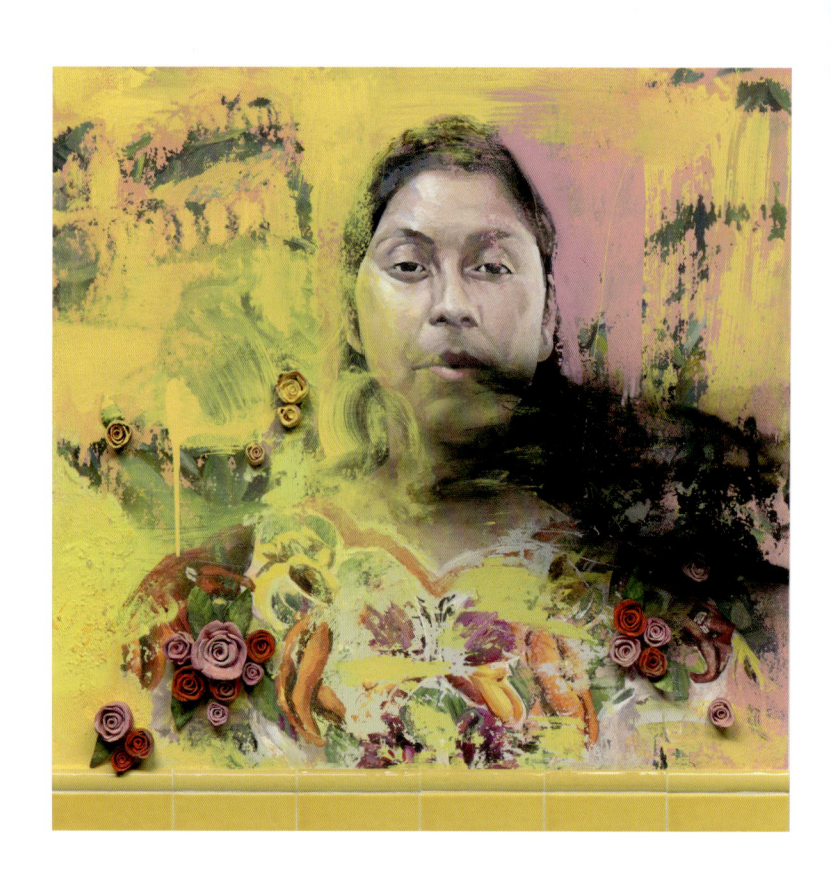

Claudia Patricia Gómez González (Reminder to Remember)

Patrick Martinez (Los Angeles, California)
Ceramic, ceramic tile, and stucco on wood,
91.4 × 91.4 × 11.4 cm (36 × 36 × 4½ in.), 2018
Collection of Arthur Lewis and Hau Nguyen

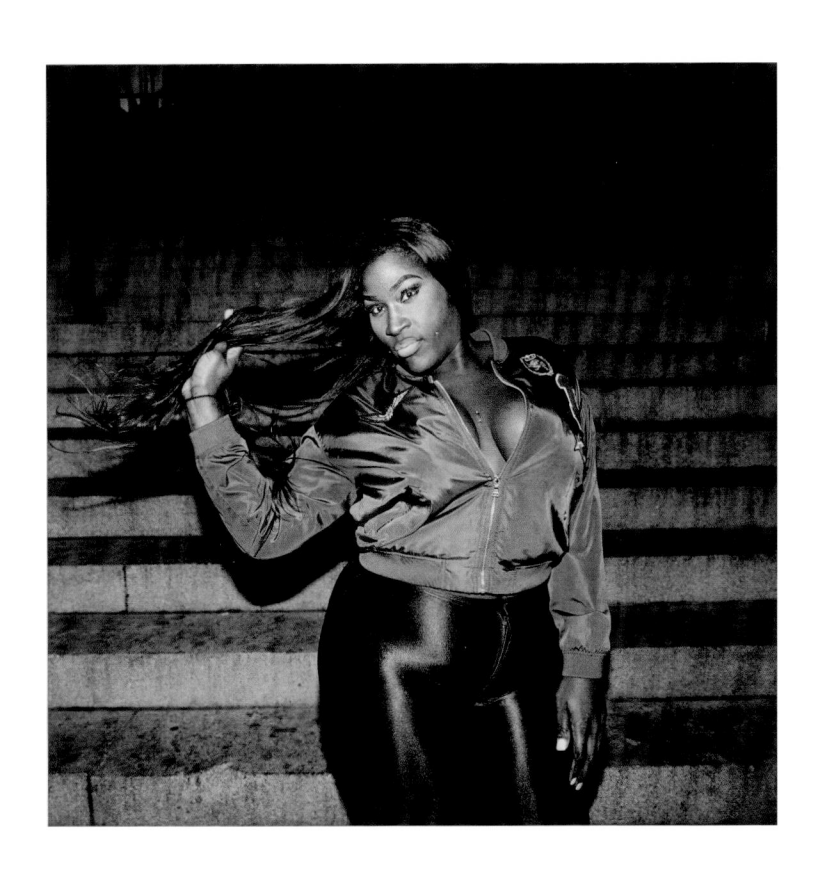

Nikki in Chinatown

Louie Palu (Washington, D.C.)
Gelatin silver print, 45.1 × 45.1 cm (17¾ × 17¾ in.), 2018
Collection of the artist

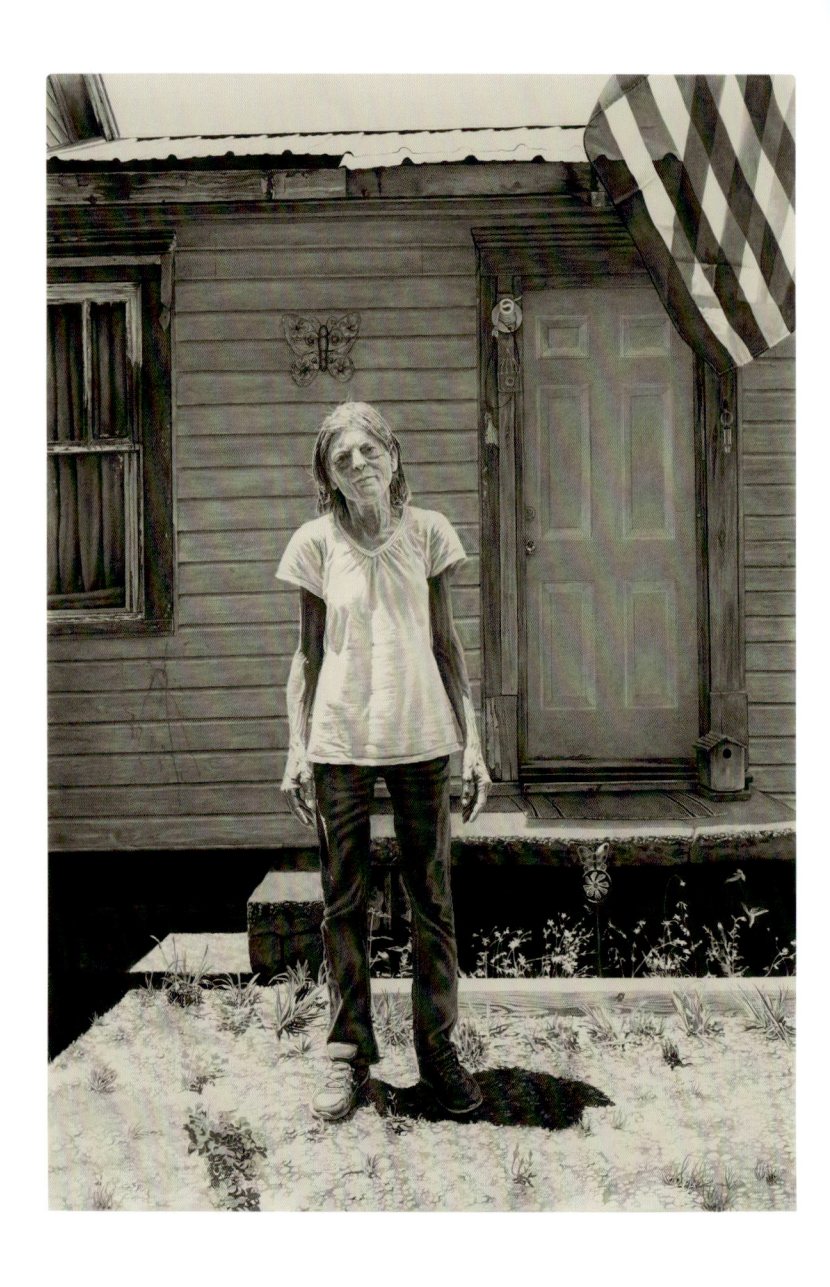

Josephine / Rest Haven Motel

Joel Daniel Phillips (Tulsa, Oklahoma)
Charcoal and graphite on paper, 155.9 × 106.7 cm (61 3/8 × 42 in.), 2017
Fort Wayne Museum of Art, Indiana; museum purchase

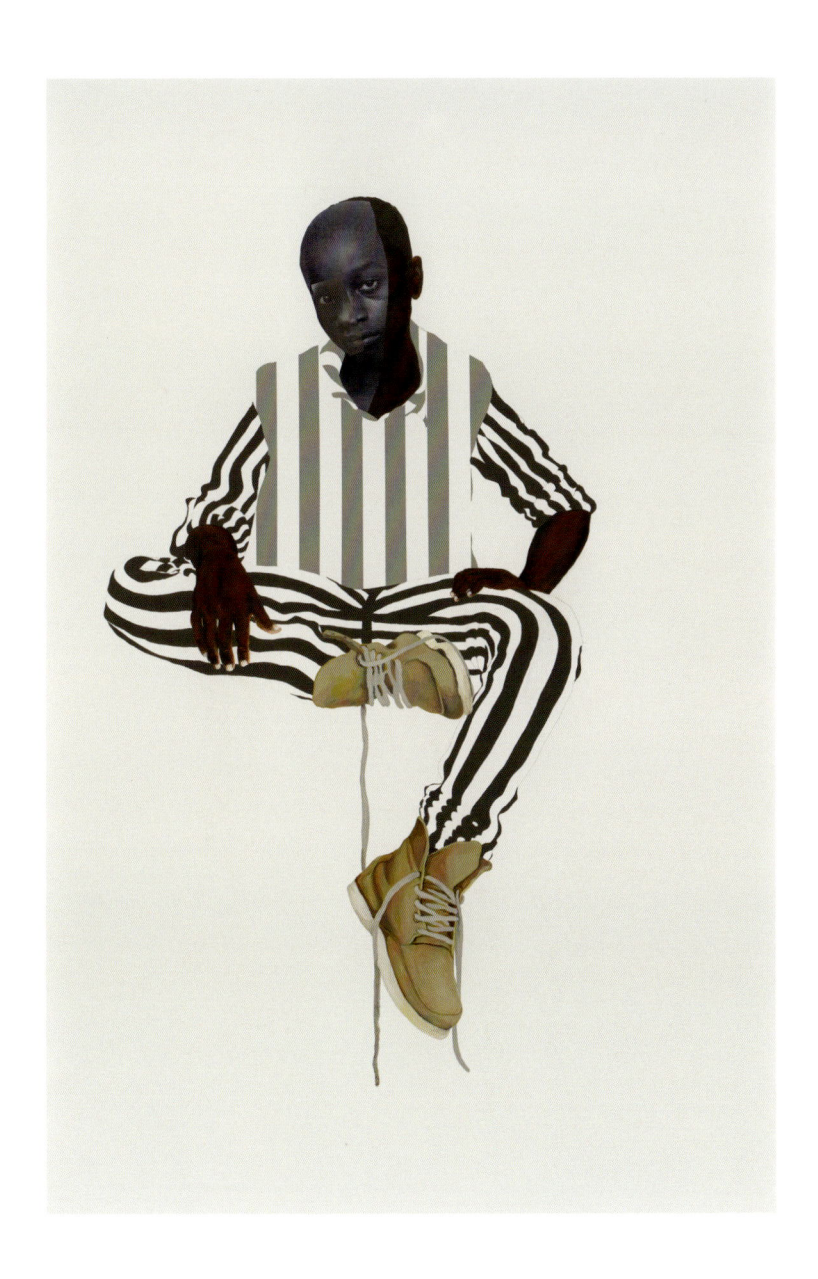

80 days (from "Nessun Dorma" series)

Deborah Roberts (Austin, Texas)
Paper, acrylic paint, graphite, and pastel on canvas,
183.5 × 122.2 cm (72¼ × 48⅛ in.), 2018
Collection of the artist, courtesy of Stephen Friedman Gallery, London

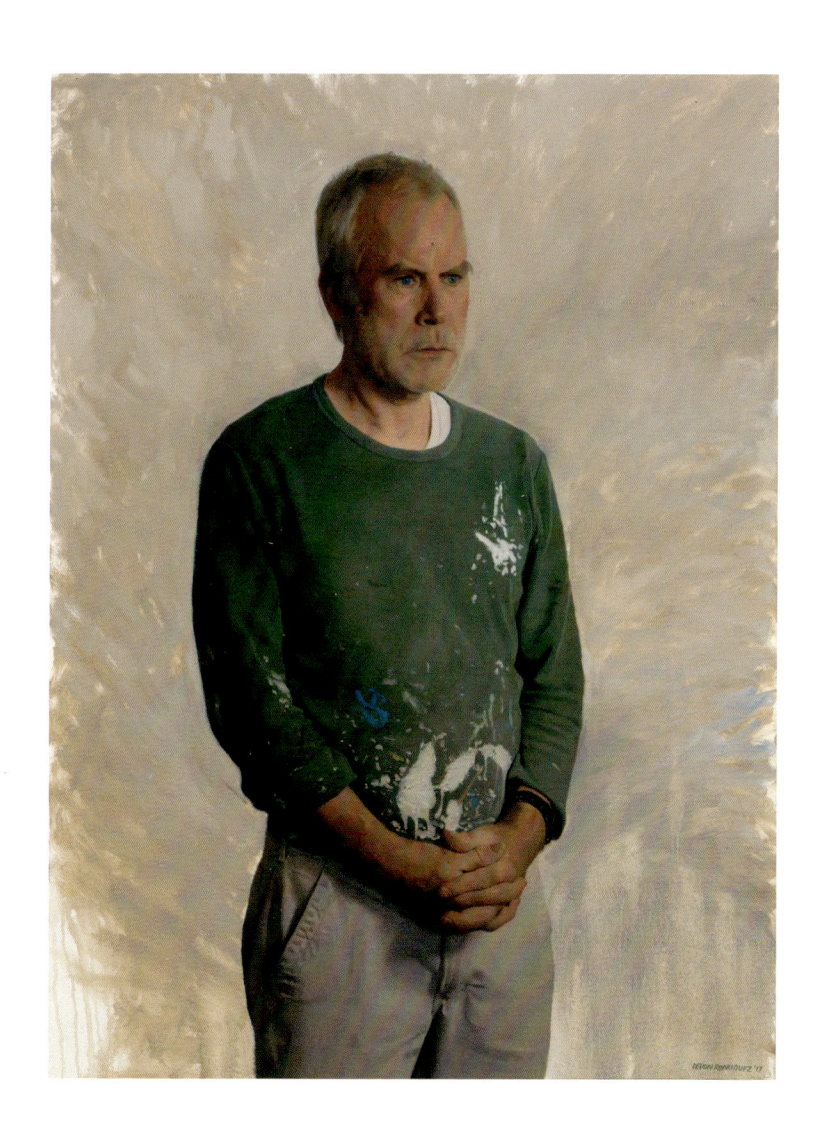

John Ahearn

Devon Rodriguez (Bronx, New York)
Oil on canvas, 101.6 × 76.2 cm (40 × 30 in.), 2017
Collection of the artist

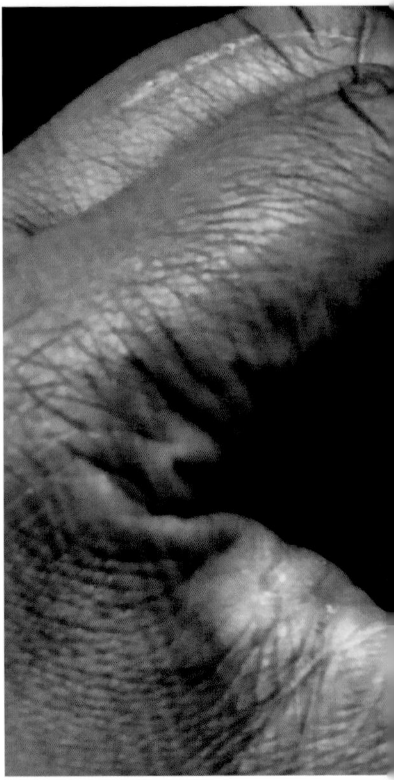

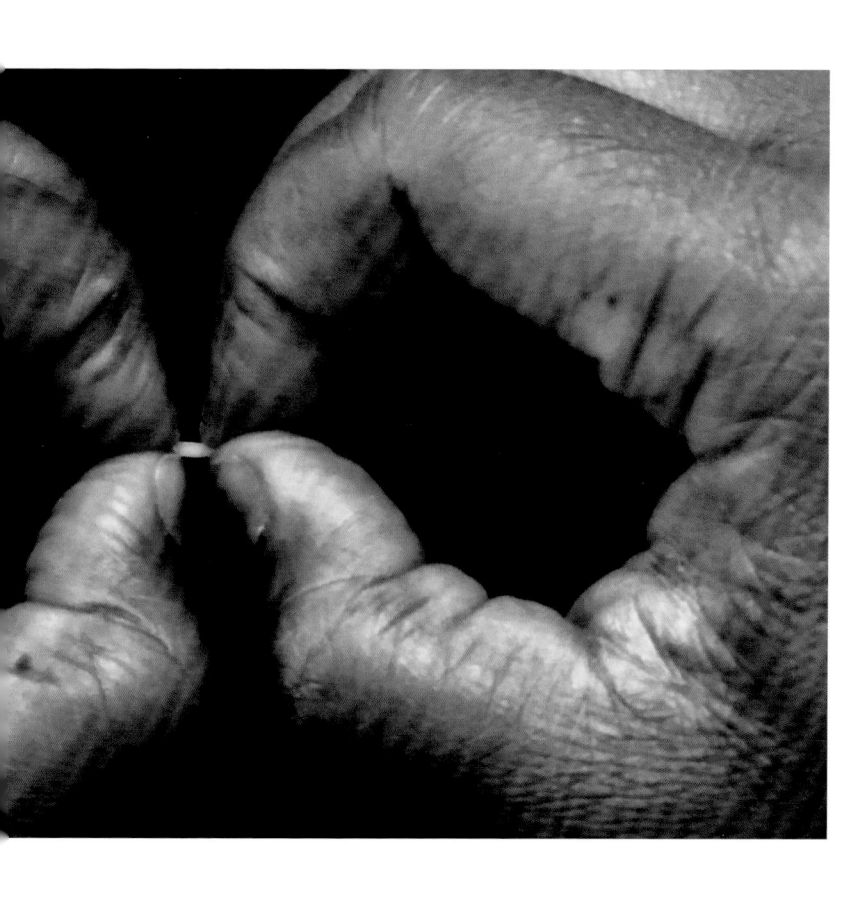

Portrait: No. 1 Man

Sheldon Scott (Washington, D.C.)
Performance with rice and HD video (approx. 13 hours), 2018
Collection of the artist, courtesy of CONNERSMITH

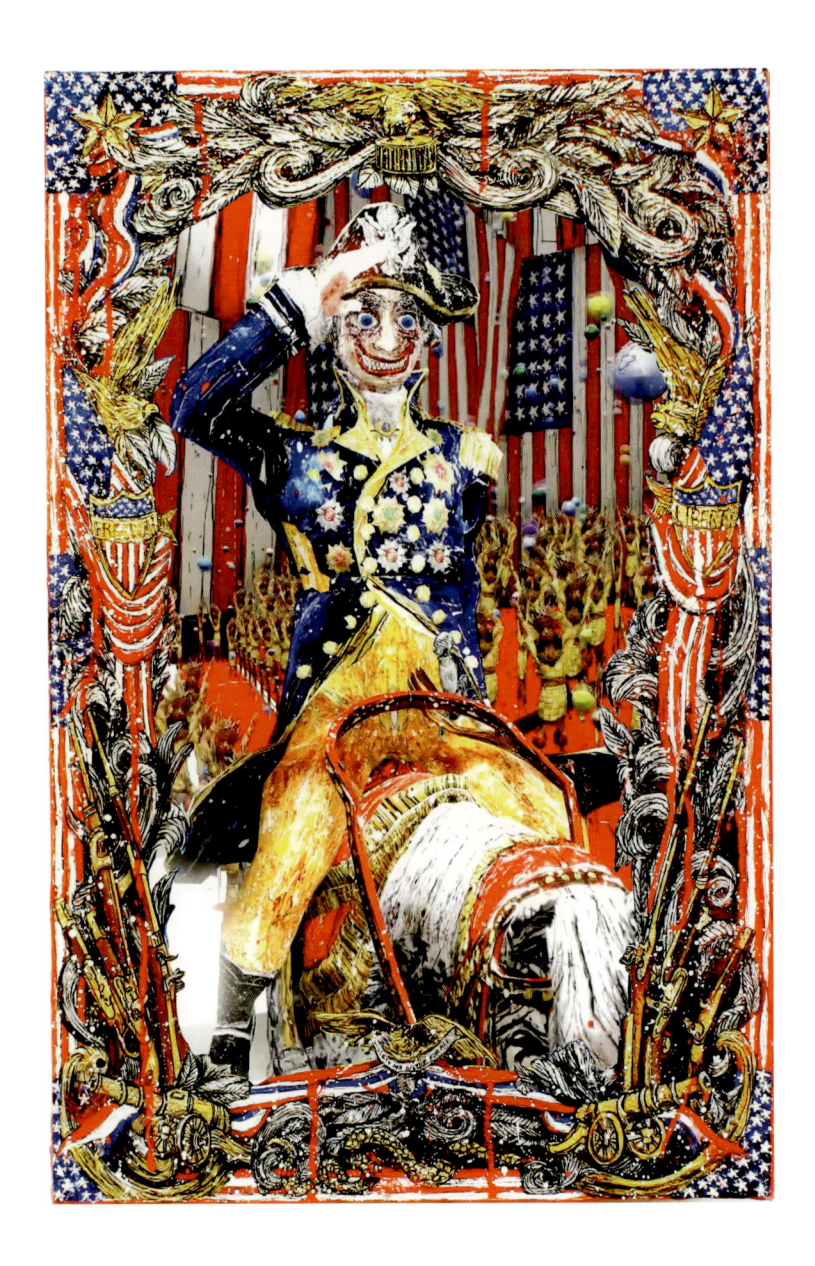

The Liberator

Federico Solmi (Brooklyn, New York)
Multimedia video, plexiglass, and acrylic paint (1:57 min.),
61.3 × 40.6 × 9.5 cm (24 1/8 × 16 × 3 3/4 in.), 2015/2016
Collection of the artist; courtesy of Luis De Jesus Los Angeles,
and Ronald Feldman Gallery, New York

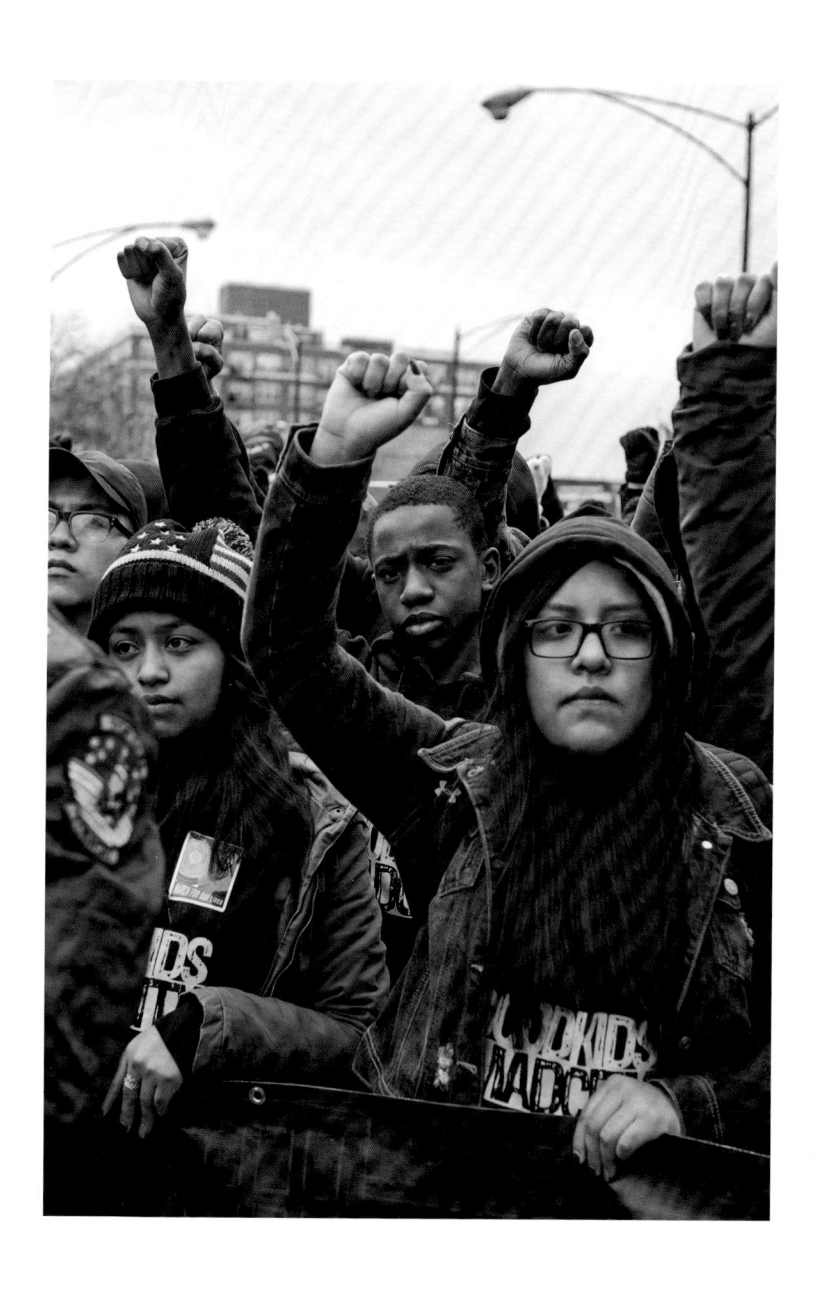

Frontline, March for Our Lives, Chicago

Sandra Steinbrecher (Chicago, Illinois)
Inkjet print, 50.8 × 33.8 cm (20 × 13 5/16 in.), 2018
Collection of the artist

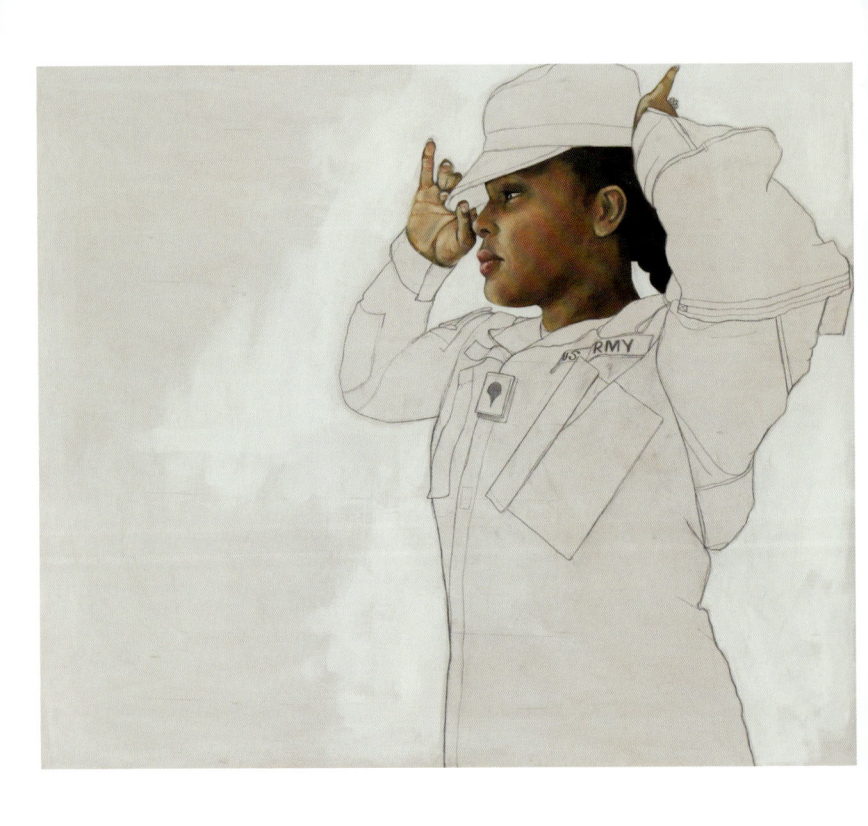

Specialist Murphy

Julianne Wallace Sterling (Albany, California)
Oil and graphite on wood, 127 × 152.4 cm (50 × 60 in.), 2016
Collection of the artist

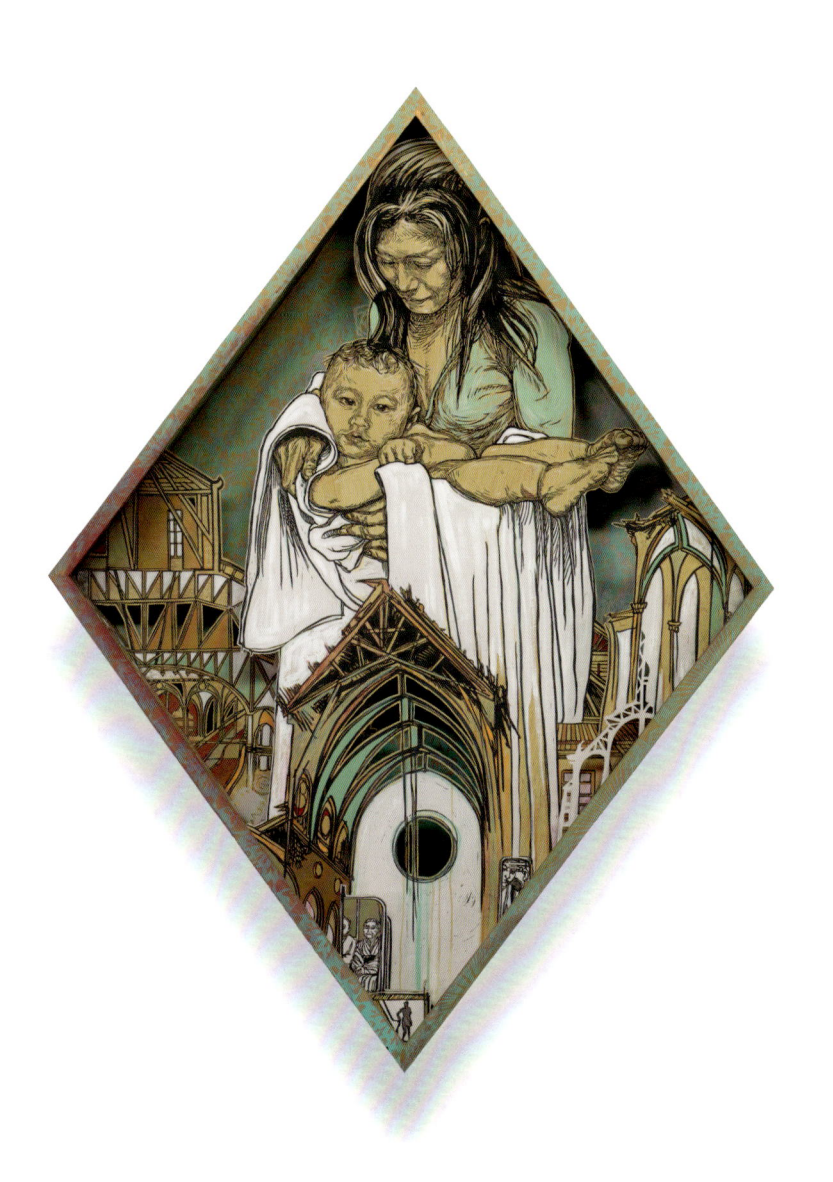

Sasu and Kasei

Swoon (Caledonia Curry) (Brooklyn, New York)
Block print, screenprint, gouache, and cut paper in artist's frame,
211.5 × 162.2 × 35.2 cm (83 1/4 × 63 7/8 × 13 7/8 in.), 2017
Collection of the artist

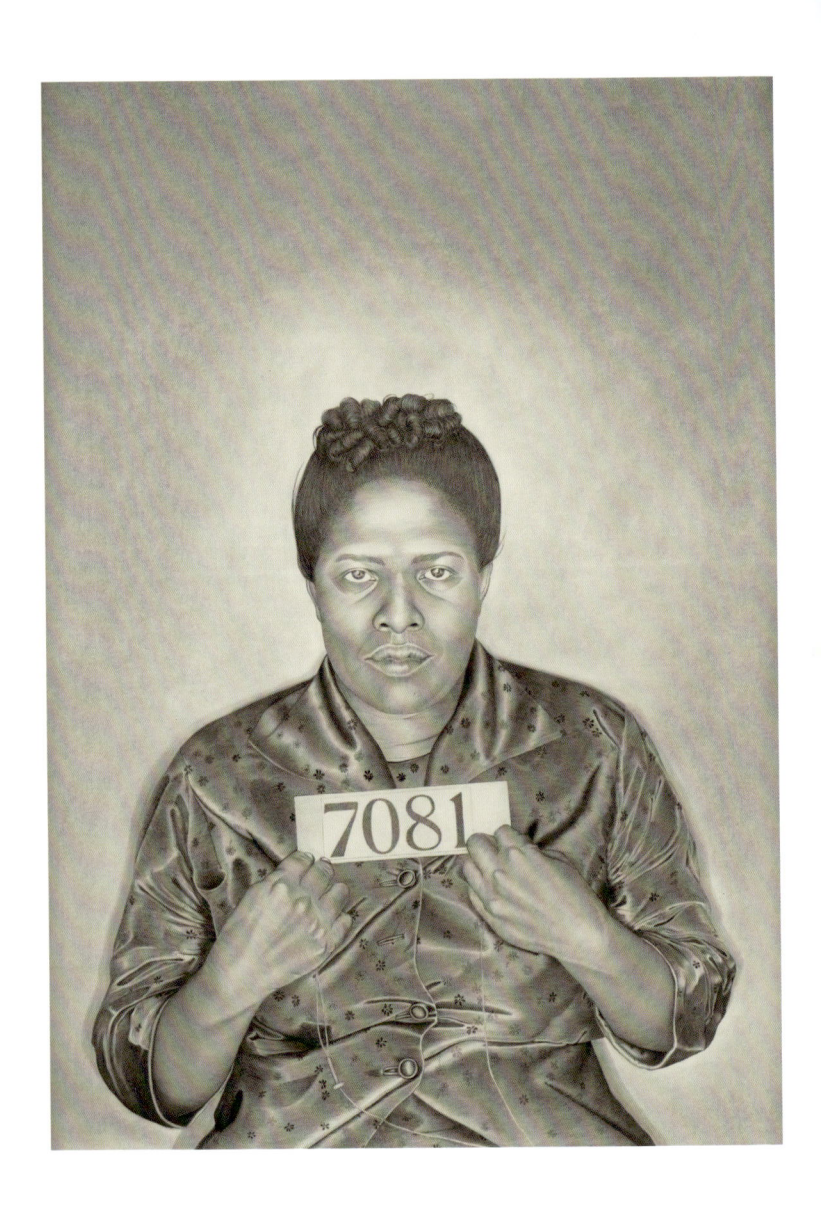

Lottie Green Varner

Lava Thomas (Berkeley, California)
Graphite and conté crayon on paper, 118.7 × 83.8 cm (46 ¾ × 33 in.), 2018
Collection of David and Pamela Hornik

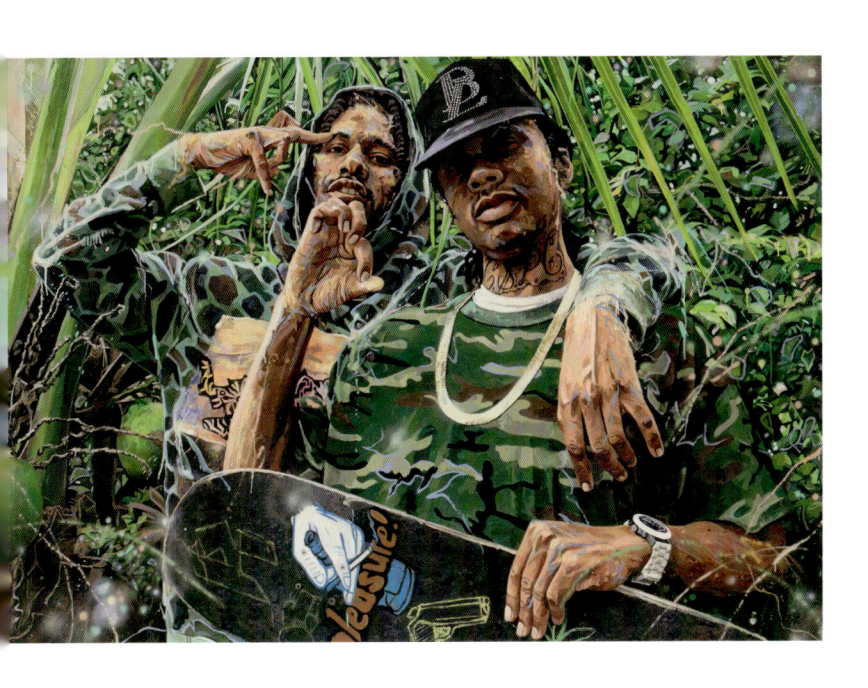

CSPG: Southway Zoo — Tropical Boyz

Michael Vasquez (Miami, Florida)
Acrylic paint and acrylic spray paint on canvas,
147 × 213.4 cm (57⅞ × 84 in), 2016
The Dean Collection

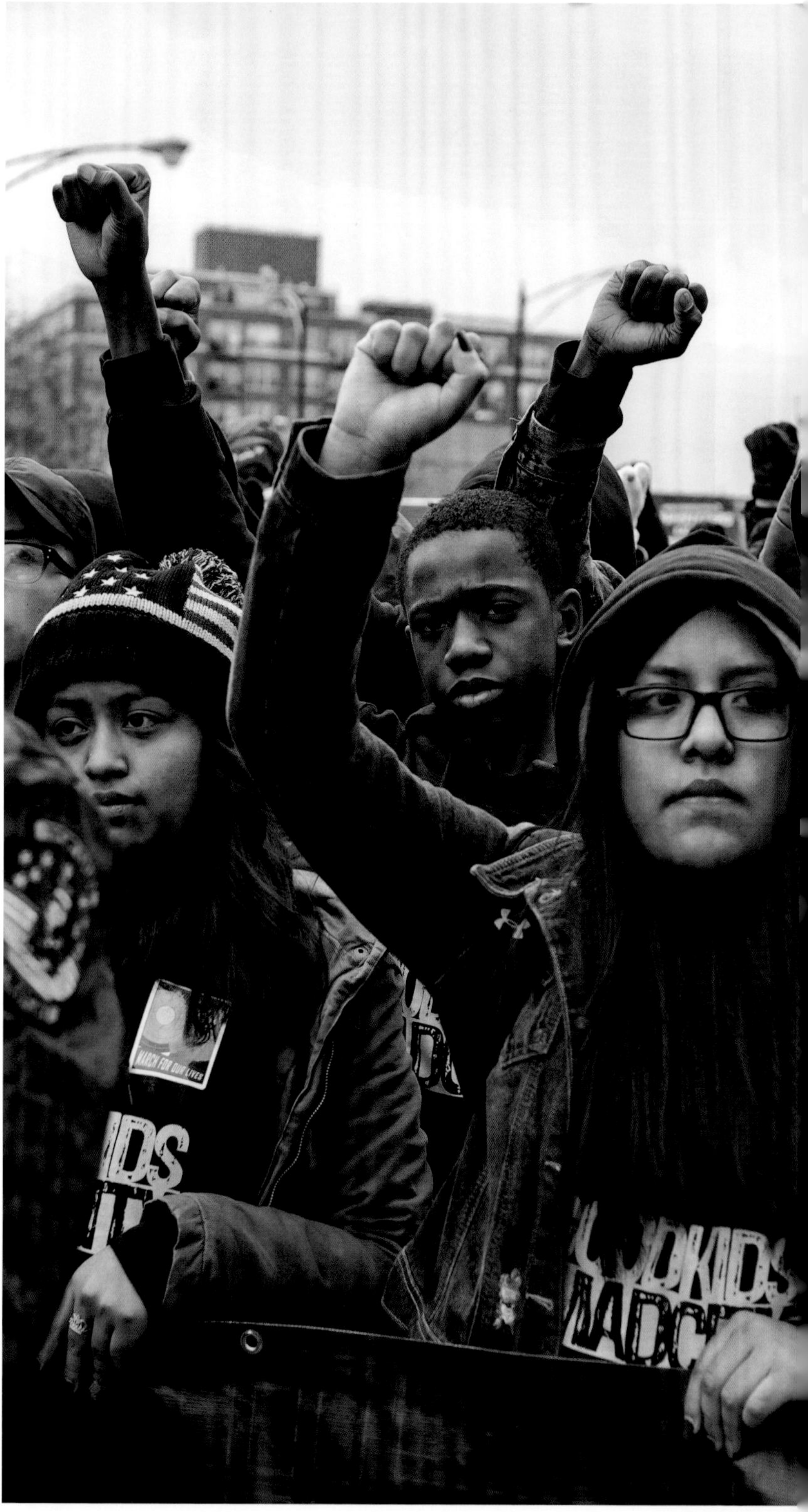
MARCH FOR OUR LIVES

Jurors' Comments

Taína Caragol

As a curator at the National Portrait Gallery, each iteration of *The Outwin: American Portraiture Today* that I have seen has been surprising in its own way, and as a first-time juror, I found the selection process to be fascinating. Unlike our other temporary exhibitions, this is a show that comes together through submissions from an open call, so the result is always eclectic. The wide range of artworks precludes the thematic or aesthetic uniformity that is often the starting point of a museum presentation, and yet, connections and common threads are inevitable.

Artists this year were encouraged to interpret the concept of portraiture broadly and to consider how it can serve as a platform to discuss the social and political issues of our time. Within those parameters, the recurrence of certain topics in the works submitted was revealing of the current concerns with which Americans are grappling. Stories cover such topics as migration, the bonds between parents and children, the vulnerability of the country's youth, and the contributions of the country's workers and veterans. I marvel at the abilities of the selected artists to disentangle complex issues from the political rhetoric that surrounds them and shed light on how they affect real individuals.

Brandon Brame Fortune

I've had the opportunity to serve on the jury for the Outwin Boochever Portrait Competition since it began in 2006. As the competition has evolved, it has been exciting to see how portraiture is becoming increasingly central as a genre that artists use to explore issues of identity and representation. All of the work selected is visually powerful and reflects the artists' deep engagement with craft as well as with their subjects. When visitors experience the historical portraits in our permanent collection galleries, they often encounter one portrait that provides a portal into an aspect of our shared history, or an entry point for exploring the context for an important event or social movement. Through portraiture, we learn about history one person at a time. The same is true, in a sense, when looking at the works in *The Outwin 2019*. An artist's focus on one person, or on a small group, can allow us to think about recent events or engage us in a larger national contemporary conversation. It is always exhilarating to be part of the process of finding those special portraits that open up our minds to larger issues or that focus our attention on what it is to live as an individual right now.

Harry Gamboa Jr.

I believe that a great portrait will follow you once you've left the gallery; the image will follow you and reverberate in your memory. The incredible artists included in *The Outwin 2019* were able to imagine their subjects and manifest the resulting imagery to later be incorporated into the actuality of the subject.

Many of these portraits invoke a direct emotional response, something that might cause an emotional response, or a memory of a previous emotional response. Quite often, the works with the ability to invoke emotions are those deemed most impressive, not only theoretically and conceptually, but they're impressive because they've been able to actually make an impression upon the viewer.

The works that stood out included those that display unique contemporary conditions, such as the portraits of workers who toil under the threat of deportation or military veterans who have defended our country. Others were those that portray individuals who have undergone various forms of physical, mental, or emotional hardship. All of these works, on some level, involve valor, bravery, and commitment in making this world a better experience. Portraiture is about honoring the person while valuing them, and at the same time, it is about understanding that we — the viewers — are making a contribution to the world.

Lauren Haynes

As a curator of contemporary art, I was very excited to see so many unique works submitted for the 2019 Outwin Boochever Portrait Competition. It's a truly valuable opportunity. One of the great things about working with living artists is that they're growing and expanding as they bring new materials into their work. This competition grants us an opportunity to take a snapshot of the art that is being made today, and it shows that our traditional view of portraiture has an opportunity to evolve with new technologies, mixed media, and performance and installation aspects.

A portrait is no longer defined as a traditional painting or photograph. Portraits are really about the feelings that arise when one is able to see into another person's life story. A good portrait may be defined as one that is technically well done, one where the artist has clearly mastered their craft and technique, but a great portrait requires a deeper connection between the viewer and the subject. Many of the strongest entries in this competition portray individuals who tend to remain behind the scenes. The finalists, in many ways, reflect where we are right now as a country, as a people.

Byron Kim

When I'm judging portraits, I am really focusing on searching for individuality — something that is idiosyncratic and distinguishes itself from the rest, something exceptional. The really great portraits are the ones that capture a sense of individuality while still conveying a powerful message or establishing a connection with the viewer.

It has been an honor to be here as a painter and bring a unique viewpoint to the judging. As a painter, I especially welcomed all of the different mediums that were represented throughout this competition. I don't think that the newer mediums, such as performance and video, are signs that portraiture is changing. Rather, I think that these different mediums in art are all becoming equally relevant.

The judging team worked very well together, and we were able to come to a consensus on the majority of our decisions. We all agreed on the artist who should win first place and felt that Hugo Crosthwaite's technique, medium, and subject matter were incredibly strong and moving. We also found consensus in concluding that photography was a very strong medium this year, so photography is very well represented in the exhibition.

Dorothy Moss

As director of the Outwin Boochever Portrait Competition, a role I took on in 2013, I am mindful of the ways in which the competition has evolved. The National Portrait Gallery makes modifications to its call for entries so it can stay in tune with the current state of portraiture and attract leading contemporary artists. This year's competition was the first to explicitly ask those who entered to respond to the current cultural and political moment. It was also the first time we departed from the mandate for direct encounters between the artist and the sitter. By adjusting the guidelines, we were able to engage with some of today's most influential portraiture artists.

    The work that rose to the top in this competition reveals a commitment to the history of representation and to bringing to light those who are most vulnerable in society or who have been relegated to the margins. Whether the artists submitted work about historical figures or represented unsung heroes of everyday life, or whether the artists honored people who are working to lead social justice movements, the work that stood out is not only brilliantly executed but also feels urgent in terms of its insistence on the presence of the subject.

Jefferson Pinder

As a juror, I am most impressed with art that is about something and with artists who are sensitive enough to know that we need more than a pretty picture right now. I'm looking for artworks that are about humanity, and I'm interested in art that addresses how individuals interact within society. With so many well-trained artists in the world, expertise is no longer enough. This is the time for risks to be taken. I look for portraits that can initiate a conversation about something deep or that begin to unravel something that is hard to put your finger on. It's about the artist addressing an issue and taking on the herculean task of being able to prompt a dialogue without being physically present with their work of art.

    For me, a good portrait connects with others by starting a conversation and allowing the viewer to finish it. You know good portraiture when you see it because it touches you; it moves you. I'm interested in the flux of change that is happening within portraiture. I struggle to clearly define portraiture because I believe we are always continuing to expand its definition as we do with this competition and exhibition and as artists continue to make portraits.

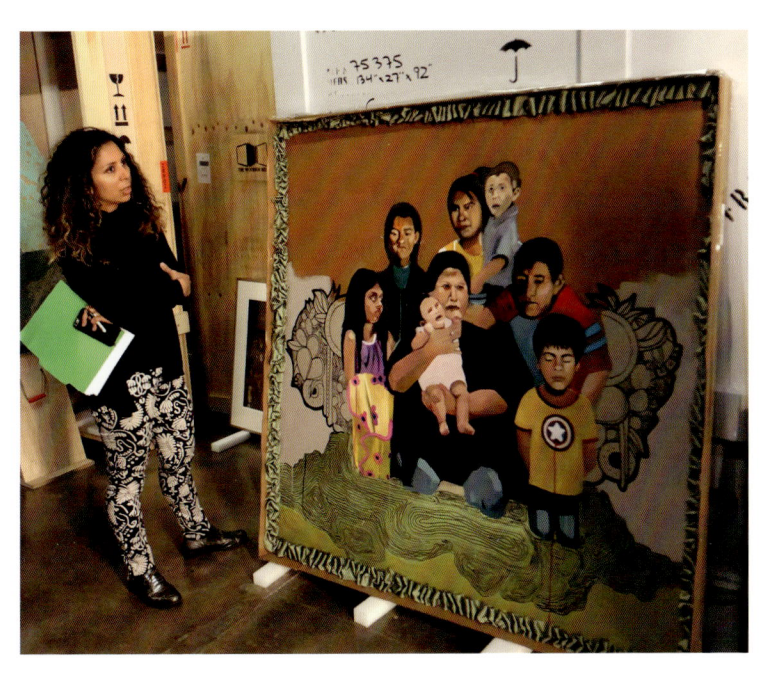

Taína Caragol, the National Portrait Gallery's curator of painting and sculpture and Latino art and history, stands next to *Desaparecidos en el Río Bravo (Disappeared in the Río Bravo)*, by Ruth Leonela Buentello, on jury day, April 15, 2019

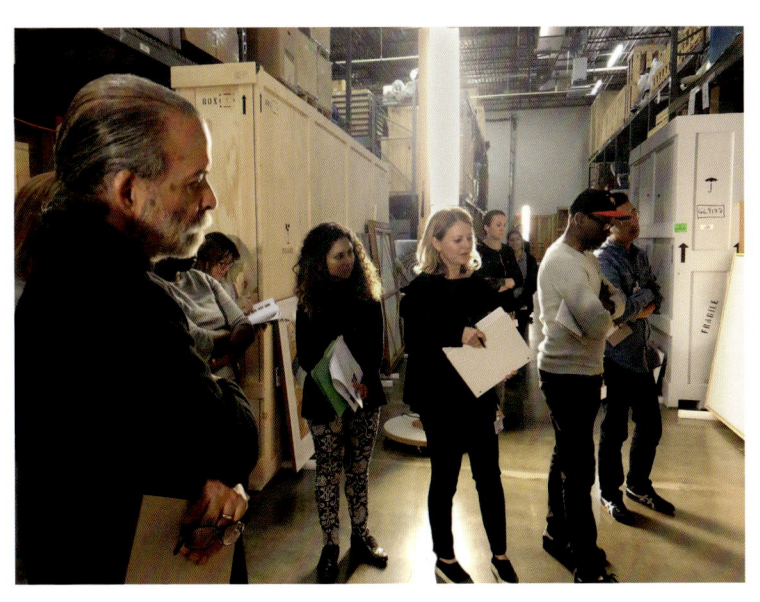

Jurors review work by semifinalists on jury day, April 15, 2019
Left to right: Harry Gamboa Jr., Taína Caragol, Dorothy Moss, Jefferson Pinder, and Byron Kim

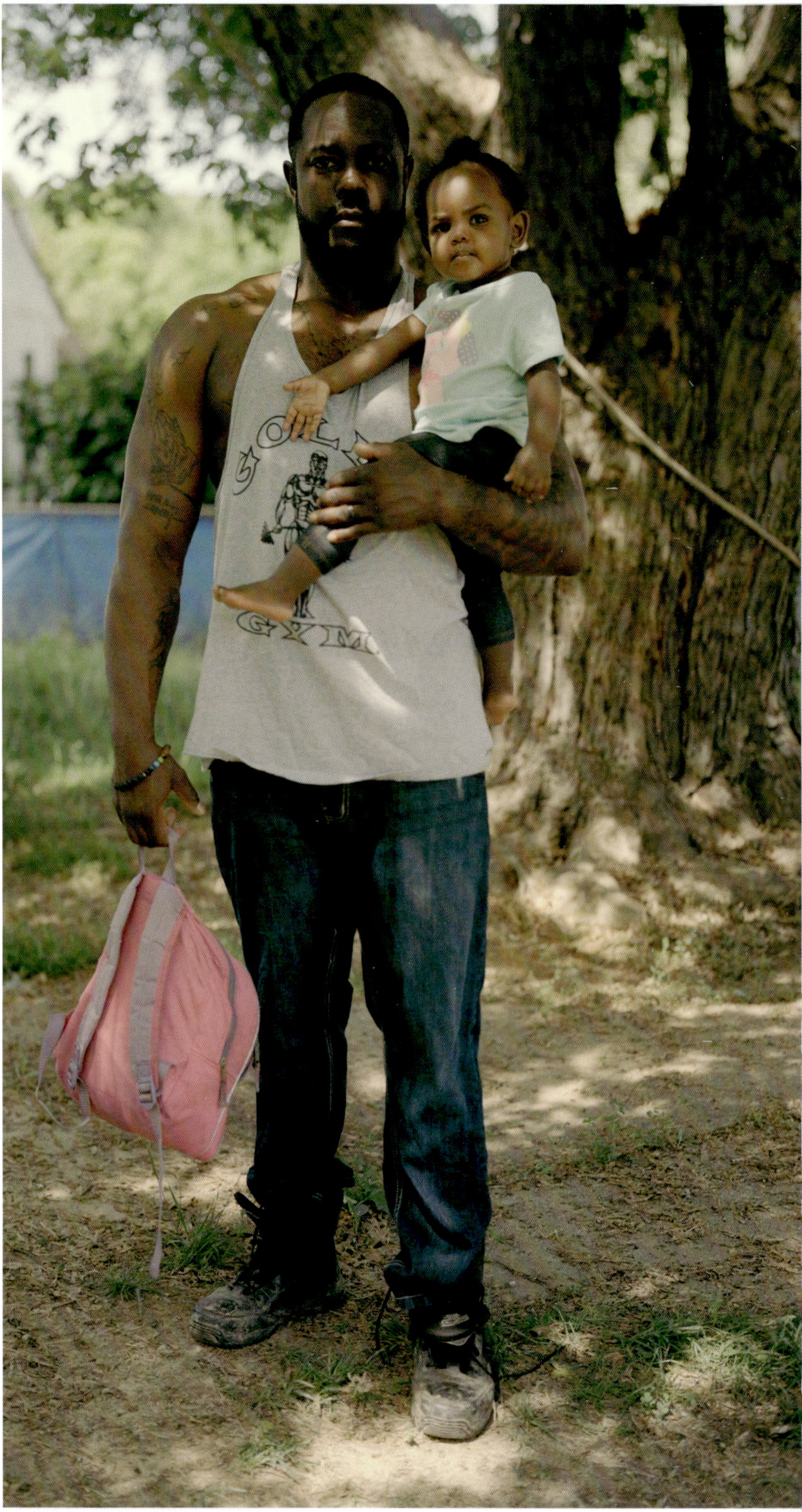

Acknowledgments

Dorothy Moss, *Curator of Painting and Sculpture, and Director, Outwin Boochever Portrait Competition, National Portrait Gallery*

This exhibition celebrates the artists, art workers, and patrons who share an unwavering commitment to the art of portraiture. I would first like to recognize the late Virginia Outwin Boochever, who endowed this exhibition and whose generous spirit ensures that portraiture remains a relevant and dynamic genre. We are enormously appreciative to have the support of her children and their spouses: David (Kathleen), Emily (William Dana), John (Carol), and Mary (Kevin Teare), who have offered invaluable support over the years to ensure that the competition continues its success into the future.

The National Portrait Gallery staff and many colleagues beyond the museum's walls contributed immeasurably to the success of the fifth Outwin Boochever Portrait Competition. Preparing for the selection of finalists and prizewinners involves our entire staff. I am especially grateful to my colleagues in the curatorial department who worked with me to carefully review the initial entries, particularly Brandon Brame Fortune, Taína Caragol, Robyn Asleson, Ann Shumard, and Leslie Ureña. Brandon, who serves as chief curator, launched the Outwin program in 2006, and it is an honor to be continuing her excellent work. This competition and exhibition benefited greatly from the leadership of the museum's director Kim Sajet, and I am grateful to her and to Gwendolyn DuBois Shaw, chief historian, for their insightful comments on draft texts.

Claire Kelly, head of exhibitions, supervised the many moving parts of the exhibition and deftly handled countless logistics. Marlene Harrison, traveling exhibitions coordinator, managed every aspect of the project with grace, professionalism, and collegiality. In the Office of the Registrar, Jennifer Wodzianski, Marissa Olivas, Pam Steele, Todd Gardner, Dale Hunt, and Wayne Long jumped into every challenging detail with a sense of humor and amazing skill. Tibor Waldner, Peter Crellin, Michael Baltzer, Bekah Charlston, and Caroline Wooden, in the Office of Design and Production, created an extraordinary experience for the artists and viewers through their expert design work. Alex Cooper, Mark Gulezian, and Grant Lazer in the Office of Exhibition Technology make each object look and sound beautiful. In the Office of New Media, Deb Sisum showed sensitivity toward the artists and their objects while managing the website and voting kiosk. She was joined by our brilliant Smithsonian Enterprise colleagues. While caring for the objects and their frames, conservators Lou Molnar, Christina Finlayson, and Im Chan offered invaluable guidance and expertise. In the Office of Audience Engagement, Rebecca Kasemeyer, Kaia Black, Ashleigh Coren, Vanessa Jones, Geri Provost Lyons, and Briana Zavadil White have ensured that the exhibition reaches countless visitors in sensitive and innovative ways. Concetta Duncan, head of communications, along with Karen Vidángos and Gaby Sama, managed the demands of today's fast-paced media outlets with the National Portrait Gallery's signature warmth and professionalism. I am also grateful to Kristy Snaman and Sara Mazzoleni in Special Events, who planned and implemented a celebratory party for the ages. In the Office of Advancement, my deepest thanks go to Lindsay Gabryszak, Sydney Golden, and Brandon Pinzini.

The 2019 Outwin Boochever Portrait Competition reached the public first through the work of our colleagues at CallForEntry.org, a service of WESTAF. We are grateful to Raquel Vasquez of WESTAF for ensuring that the entry process went smoothly. The staff at Crozier Fine Arts, particularly Matt Curran, Steve Morrison, Jason Mowery, and Kwok Chan, provided a wonderful space for our final jury day and offered expert assistance with the shipping, unpacking, and storage of the semifinalists' work.

This publication reflects the visions of both Margaret Bauer, who designed an exquisite book, and Rhys Conlon, who masterfully edited the manuscript and managed the catalogue's production. I am also grateful to Sarah McGavran for her thoughtful editing of the exhibition texts.

Our external jurors — Harry Gamboa Jr., Lauren Haynes, Byron Kim, and Jefferson Pinder — were a dream team. Their integrity and their commitment to the objectives of the Outwin paved the way for a compelling, thought-provoking exhibition. We are indebted to each of the jurors for their thoughtfulness in choosing the finalists and prizewinners. Their insights and expertise allowed for meaningful dialogues about contemporary portraiture to take place and made the jury experience memorable.

Several contractors, interns, and researchers contributed to this project. My heartfelt thanks go especially to Moselle Kleiner, who offered excellent suggestions in the planning stages and whose hard work strengthened the exhibition. I am also grateful to researchers Carolina Maestre and Jiete Li for brilliantly assisting with the final jury day. After the jury selection was complete, interns Sara Jewel, Sara Sims Wilbanks, and Libby Fischer played an important role in the artist research process.

My profound thanks go to Taína Caragol, co-curator of the exhibition, whose expertise in contemporary art and portraiture were invaluable in shaping the competition and exhibition. I look forward to seeing how the program develops when Taína assumes the role of director with the 2021 Outwin Boochever Portrait Competition.

As the late Toni Morrison reflected on the importance of art in divided times, she wrote: "This is *precisely* the time when artists go to work. There is no time for despair, no place for self-pity, no need for silence, no room for fear. We speak, we write, we do language. That is how civilizations heal." More than 2,600 artists took the time to answer the call for entries, and we are grateful to each of them — and to all of the individuals mentioned above — for going to work and believing in the power of portraiture.

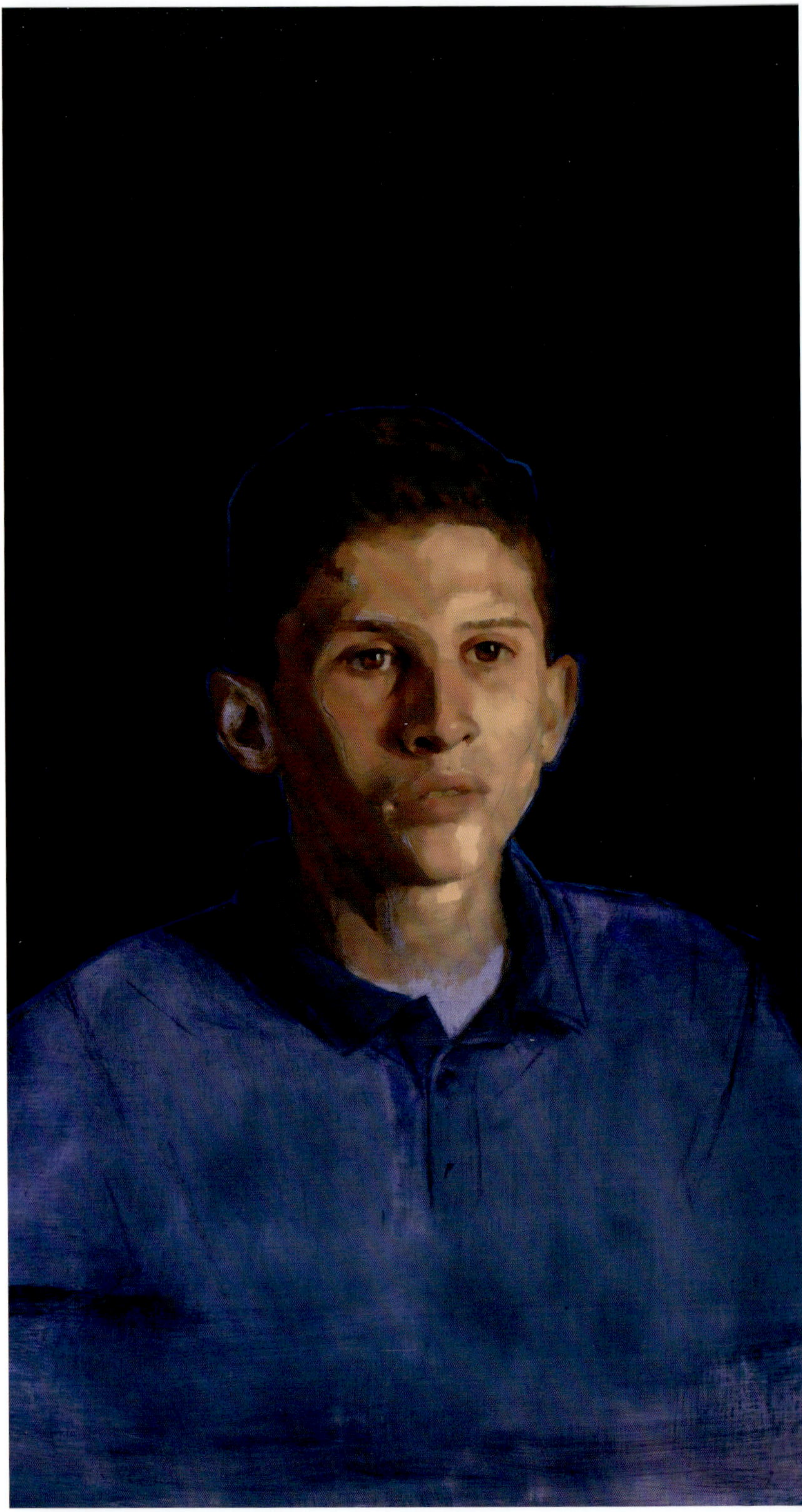

Previous Prize Winners
Outwin Boochever Portrait Competition

2006

First Prize: David Lenz, *Sam and the Perfect World*, Oil on linen, 44 × 46 in. (111.8 × 116.8 cm), 2005

Second Prize: Yuqi Wang, *From Red Hook*, Oil on linen 76.2 × 76.2 cm (30 × 30 in.), 2005

Third Prize: Nuno de Campos, *Magnet #3*, Egg tempera on linen on panel, 38.1 × 38.1 cm (15 × 15 in.), 2005

2009

First Prize: Dave Woody, *Laura*, Inkjet print, 81.3 × 63.5 cm (32 × 25 in.), 2007

Second Prize: Stanley Rayfield, *Dad*, Oil on canvas, 150.2 × 126.4 cm (59 1/8 × 49 3/4 in.), 2008

Third Prize: Adam Vinson, *Dressy Bessy Takes a Nap*, Oil on panel, 43.2 × 30.5 cm (17 × 12 in.), 2008

2013

First Prize: Bo Gehring, *Jessica Wickham*, HD video (5:05 min.), 2010

Second Prize: Jennifer Levonian, *Buffalo Milk Yogurt*, Digital video/animation (6:46 min.), 2010

Third Prize: Sequoyah Aono, *Self-Portrait*, Acrylic on wood, with steel base, height: 177.8 cm (70 in.), 2010

2016

First Prize: Amy Sherald, *Miss Everything (Unsuppressed Deliverance)*, Oil on canvas, 137.2 × 109.5 cm (54 × 43 1/8 in.), 2013

Second Prize: Cynthia Henebry, *Mavis in the Backseat*, Inkjet print, 101.6 × 127 cm (40 × 50 in.), 2013

Third Prize: Joel Daniel Phillips, *Eugene #4*, Charcoal and graphite on paper, 182.9 × 132.1 cm (72 × 52 in.), 2014

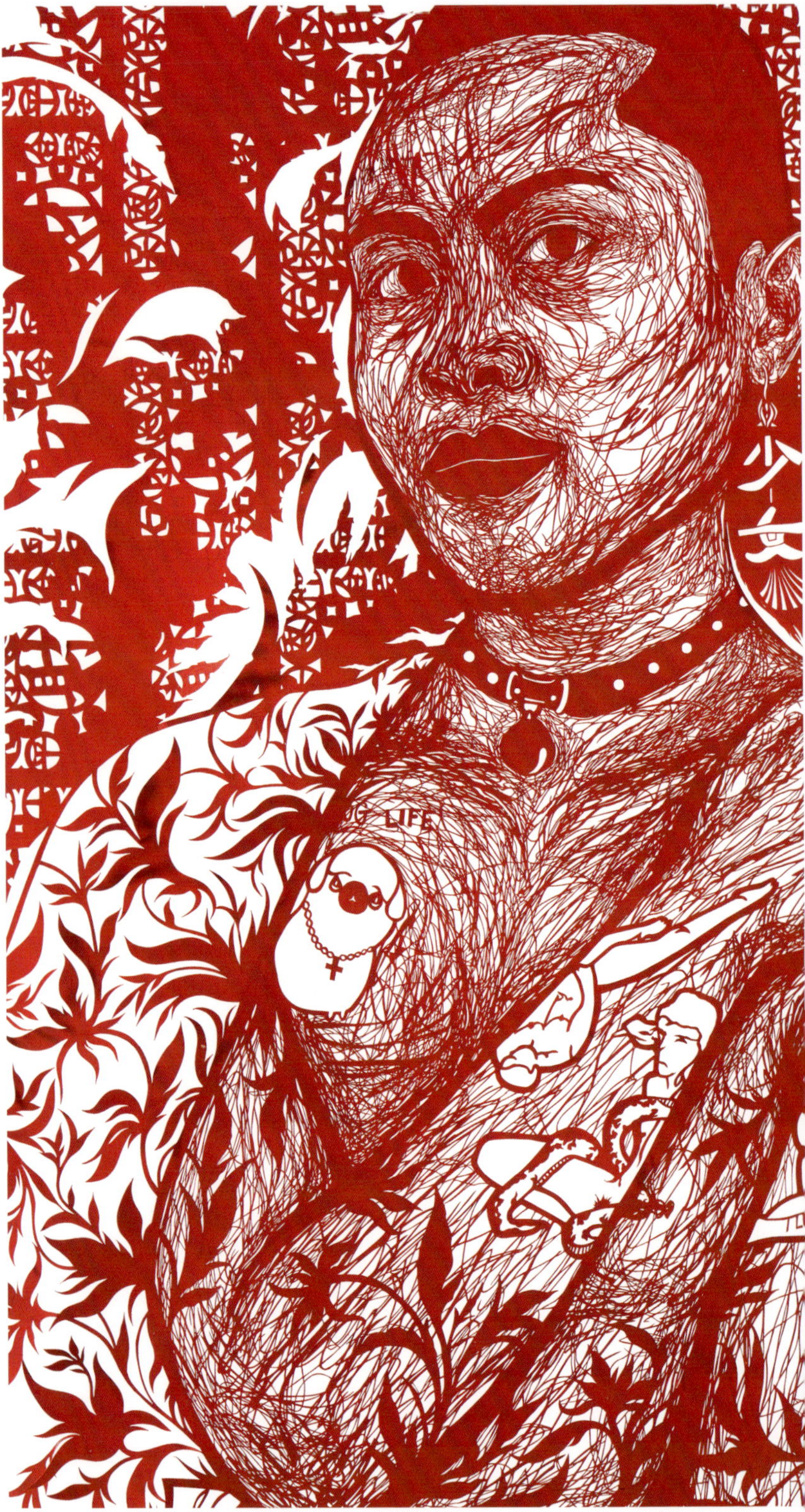
少女
LIFE

Index of Artists

ADÁL, 36
Adams, Paul, 37
Álvarez Roure, Luis, 38
Attie, Shimon, 39
Atwood, Tom, 40
Beckett, Claire, 41
Brown, Quinn Russell, 42
Buentello, Ruth Leonela, 43
Bui, Antonius-Tin, 44
Byrnside, Mike, 45
Capshaw, Kate, 46–47
Centofanti, Daniel, 48
Cogan, Joshua, 49
Comen, Sam, 26–27
Cook, Larry W., Jr., 50
Corey, Carl, 51
Crawford, Carla, 53
Crosthwaite, Hugo, 24–25
Cruz, David Antonio, 54
Diamond, Ronald, 55
Dubnau, Jenny, 56
Dugan, Jess T., 57
Durrett, Nekisha, 58–59
Faustine, Nona, 60

Gaignard, Genevieve, 61
García Clark, Natalia, 32
Garner, Anna, 62
Greene, Richard, 28–29
Hare, Lauren, 33
Huckaby, Sedrick, 63
Layton, Jordan, 37
Lee, Zun, 64–65
Lemke, William, 66–67
Martinez, Patrick, 68
McIntosh, Wayde, 30–31
Palu, Louie, 69
Phillips, Joel Daniel, 70
Roberts, Deborah, 71
Rodriguez, Devon, 73
Scott, Sheldon, 74–75
Solmi, Federico, 76
Steinbrecher, Sandra, 77
Sterling, Julianne Wallace, 78
Swoon (Caledonia Curry), 79
Thomas, Lava, 80
Vasquez, Michael, 81
Walker, Adrian Octavius, 34

Published to accompany the exhibition "The Outwin 2019: American Portraiture Today," celebrating the finalists of the fifth triennial Outwin Boochever Portrait Competition.

National Portrait Gallery, Smithsonian Institution, Washington, D.C.
October 26, 2019 – August 30, 2020

Mildred Lane Kemper Art Museum Washington University in St. Louis
January 29 – April 18, 2021

Alaska State Museum, Juneau
May 28 – September 19, 2021

For tour updates, please visit *portraitcompetition.si.edu*.

© 2019 Smithsonian Institution

All images are © the artist. Photography © Pete Souza: fig. 1, p. 12. Photography © Jim Gipe: p. 8. Photography © Kim Sajet: p. 87. Photography supplied by finalists: pp. 22, 25, 27, 29, 32–34, 36, 39–42, 45, 48–51, 57, 60, 62, 64–65, 74–77, 82, and 88. All other photography by Mark Gulezian,

© National Portrait Gallery, Smithsonian Institution.

Details: p. 2 (Álvarez Roure); p. 4 (McIntosh); p. 10 (Roberts); p. 22 (Crosthwaite); p. 82 (Steinbrecher); p. 88 (Cook); p. 92 (Capshaw); p. 94 (Bui).

Page 8: Virginia Outwin Boochever, 2001. Photograph by Jim Gipe. National Portrait Gallery, Smithsonian Institution; gift of Virginia Boochever, courtesy of Smith College

ISBN: 978-0-9786657-5-3
Library of Congress Control Number: 2019949877

Produced by the National Portrait Gallery, Smithsonian Institution

Rhys Conlon, Head of Publications

Designed by Margaret Bauer, Washington, D.C. Typeset in Zwo Pro; Printed on Sterling Matte by Meridian Printing, East Greenwich, Rhode Island

The spellings of names (with or without accents) adhere to each individual's preferences.